Table of Contents

The Beginning

Herein the reader will be presented with a range of historical influential figures, these stories reflect the development of symbols through compressed account of some of the world's most prominent and celebrated geniuses of all times. Among these are some of the most famous and dedicated interdisciplinary expert scientists, renowned creative artists and cultural figures, as well as ancient and modern literary philosophical giants. The inadequacy of this written account falls short of rendering a precise and complete overview of all of history's big thinkers and spectacular creative minds. Many thousands of more like-minded people are not mentioned herein, they likewise attested to a universal truth and contributed in all fields of human endeavors. They too deserve recognition for their emancipation of rational reason, logic and dignified unfathomable human experience which they confronted their peers within excess of the social affairs of their time. The multiplicity of individual worlds described in these words, aims to emphasize the unique traits of these venerated men and women and the universality of ways with which their arbitrary characters have distinguished them.

The breathtaking words and actions of these humans have set them apart from the rest of us and propagated their legacies through the echoes of time. During the unfolding of history critical ontological reports have surfaced, regarding the many evident personal similarities which have transpired in the lives of many of these creative geniuses. Needless to say, these humans collectively broke the mold of social order and norms of normal behavior. The creative trademarks of these individuals, has in many instances, been accompanied by simultaneous instances of psychological and physical personal suffering. Their perceptual capacity to view the world around them, and deduct truth from the essence of reality, in original and novel ways, also bestowed upon them eccentric behaviors and perplexing signs of mental illness. These "tortured geniuses" that achieved the mental exercise of "thinking outside the box," also concurrently exhibited signs of mental dualities in many cases. These traits have in many regards, attributed them with antisocial behaviors with irreducible differences of mind, such for which a tolerance did not prevail in the general population around them during their lifetime. Societies at large have through historic development passed antagonistic judgement on patterns of abnormal behavior and unique self-differentiations.

Our fears for the unknown remain a distrusting paradox, it is an inconsistent instinct which oscillates between our rational understanding of our own ego, and the renouncing of the common need and necessity for the betterment of the human condition. Our misconception of the natural progression of creative processes and efforts, which are evident in the lives of these people, have been at times labeled as; incomprehensible, mad and crazy. Yet those very same individuals, have time and time again proven to us, that our collective ignorance triumphs even beyond our reason and logic when confronted with the brave intellectual complexity of a genius. Regardless of the countless debilitating cognitive conditions such subjects have endured, we must not only uphold our empathy for their psychological suffering. But we should also, cherish and exemplify them with high regards, the many sacrifices that they evidently carried as unimaginable burdens to their persona in their quest for increasing our common knowledge and examination of reality indeed became actualized ideals. Their inquiry, into the existential richness, of the mind and the cosmos, the earth and all the glorious manifestation of life, the evidence regarding their struggles for wisdom and knowledge are unmistakably made abundantly clear for all of us to observe.

Albeit constrained by space and time, our thoughts, beliefs, and our actions have in all instances of our social, economic, ethical and political life been affected with benefits in numerous ways from their legacy. These people have collectively ushered in the scientific revolution and revolutionized our possibility structures, acts which none of us could have imagined our conceived of on our own. The brilliance of these individuals has amounted to a cognitive ascension, which hardly can be summarized or expressed adequately by any one person. The unification of cultures has truly been enacted through the vast plentitude of records that have been kept on their lives, this is the foundation of knowledge which our future generations will inherit. For every piece of discovery that they made, equally much or more has sadly been lost along the way. Humanity is hence faced with acknowledgement of past judgment and injustice which was forced upon other geniuses against their knowledge and intuitions, this forever will remain a transgression which we collectively must reconcile. We ought to respect to what extreme degree these individuals were afflicted by their contemporaries, circumstantial situations and power edifices which imposed inevitable obstacles and threats on their intelligence and states of mind.

As we now try to distinguish the correlation between creativity and pathological obsessions with grandiose goals towards greatness, we must adhere to our own cognitive struggles when defining these same indistinguishable limits. Boundaries which we otherwise may perceive as valid, should remain subordinate to mere eccentric patterns of personality as opposed to classified clinical personality disorders. With an ever-evolving understanding of our sociology, the German philosopher Jürgen Habermas defined our lives in two different worlds, a systemworld and a lifeworld. In the latter we as humans adhere to spontaneous dialogue with other people, this is the kind of world that existed particularly as an example within society before the dawn of the emergence of the modern welfare states in Scandinavian countries. Citizens earlier enjoyed free conversations with their peers within their public discourse, as such the dialogue was not dominated by any external actors. Concurrently, this lifeworld in most Western societies has effectively been utterly deconstructed (colonized) by what he deemed as the systemworld. This system is composed mainly by the capitalist means of production and public governance through heavy bureaucratic tools.

Hence a dismantling of privacy and our personal sphere of communication and actions has emerged, it arises through the all-encompassing economic system which has replaced the public sphere with a dominating administration system of public affairs. Consequently, the society as a whole has become embedded within the professionalization and specialization of knowledge whereby a wedge is erected between bureaucrats, experts and researchers on one side and the general population on the other. Hence a remarkable opposition seen between administrative and political positions in governance of local, regional or national offices, is the hallmark of these two worlds not communicating with one another. The extended ramifications, of the lack of discourse, further distances the common good of societal development away from citizens and those individuals in power positions. As such, the logic of domination in the systemworld evolves through a sectorized mindset of governance instead of being guided by the cultural collective will of the lifeworld. It befalls us therefore to recognize as members of any society, with humility and awe, that our knowledge of the human mind in all its marvelous emergent features, still remains predominantly in the realm of fiction and uncertainty.

It is only with recent advancements in neuroscience and cognitive psychology, that we have finally begun to yield answers and to shed light on the myriad of mysteries that we barely have scratched the surface of. It is as such, an unflattering attempt which still may prove impossible to communicate with political correctness, and to analyze with efficacy as we try to impose a diagnosis on ourselves or dare to criticize posthumously many of these great individuals spoken of in this book. Although educated guesses have been presented by researchers regarding their conditions. It is hence nevertheless prudent of the reader, to re-normalize his or her own perception of the social regulations within which they currently exist, and to do so knowingly, before passing any judgement on the properties of others which cannot be reduced unto themselves. This vital question remains; how our modern world can learn from these extraordinary people? As we are only now starting to understand that the high levels of intelligence such people exhibit, seem to imply, that highly intelligent persons are more at risk of developing mental illness. This occurrence implies a correlated validity, as seemingly their mind and body display a diminished filtering in somatic, visual and auditory stimulus from the environment, and a heightened level of awareness through a hyperactive central nervous system.

Hence as such these creative geniuses have managed to expose and formulate the reality of foundational knowledge. Through such mesmerizing connections and intersections of the mind and body, these relations that so few others have, seem to maintain the elaborate cognitive traits required for revolutionary divergent thinking. The world, should remember that our current understanding of the causes for psychological disturbances ranging from clinical depression to Messiah complexes, remain predominantly not at all well understood. Despite the advent of new modern treatment methodologies, little noticeable progress has been made with successful treatments of patients suffering from a wide range of mental afflictions. Deeper insight into the conflicting and contradictory nature of a genius vs crazy person and their faculties of mind, will most likely discredit the deficits in our knowledge when trying to determine what actually is normal behaviors amongst our species. We must also adhere to facts and recall how scientific discovery has been tainted and mitigated by special interest groups, both in medical, educational and political institutions. As with regards to the development of technology in Deep Brain Stimulation (DBS) that was carried out in the 1950s, by psychiatrist Robert Heath, who was the first to implant electrodes deep in the brain of subjects.

The aim was then set, to research whereas a profound impact on the human sense of self, could be discovered while measuring pleasure. Those efforts were carried out, with good intentions and with clear relevant empirical results, as being a promising technology that could have changed modern psychiatry for good. Well over a half a century later, the scientific community stood in awe, when the pioneer Elon Musk revealed the achievements and plans of Neuralink, which stands to offer a paradigm shift in the very same field of work. Thereby, the future entails, us all with this power, not only to treat mental disorders, but it also grants us the powers to modulate our behaviors and characters. Hence, the stage is set for the final drama of humanity to play itself out, wherein we finally embody and disrupt all our illusions and delusions through scientific discovery, or we simply embark on a journey of artificial culture creation. This then remains the shameful acknowledgement which we must bear as a species, that we must arise from our unconscious slumber or remain trapped in the ontological nightmare of our own construct. Our community parity of peaceful coexistence, would obviously rather have us believe that some of us, are not in fact not capable of transcending the regular tendencies of prerequisite insight or specialization into the wisdom of our own human nature.

The false narrative is daily proclaimed, by which unconformity is not worthy of societal acceptance. The predominant stance against freedom of mind stands against us, both as we are climbing career ladders and within any formal cultural constructions if we object to current intelligent democratic narratives by referencing historical accounts. It must as such be obvious, that we as agents of free thought uphold a fractured misconception regarding a sovereign generalist and objective worldview, a view based wholly on reason, logic and personal experience. Hence the attempt to obfuscate truth from any alternate states of mind, remains a threatening instrument of corruption within the status quo of common disciplinary actions and monopoly on violence by the police. Deep politics are enforced by society through required legal compliance to competency within frameworks and structural generation of governance institutions. This irrational fear of the mind constitutes the clash of civilizations within all societies and continues to govern the dissemination of all of humanity's finest advancements by way of copyrights, patents, and trademarks of intellectual property.

The order of society does this knowingly, hence it seeks to further legitimize its exercise of power by fragmenting and narrowing all fields of personal liberty and cooperation between free minds and their desire for fundamental democratic distribution of ownership of all knowledge and truth.

< The innocent sleep, when the evils are awake >

"Great spirits have always encountered violent opposition from mediocre minds." Albert Einstein

Abraham Lincoln

(1809 - 1865) 16th president of the United States

Abraham Lincoln was America's 16th president. His term of office was from March 1861 to April 1965. He led the US through the Civil War, putting an end to slavery and a lot of internal crisis. Lincoln was an experienced State Attorney, Senator, and a member of the U.S Congress. He did everything he could, to put an end to the slave trade as president. He was the first US president to be killed. He's the greatest of all the presidents of the United States. Lincoln was popular as a local fighter, but he hated hunting and fishing as he hated killing animals.

Despite suffering from severe depression, the Great Emancipator managed to lead the country through one of its most difficult periods. One of Lincoln's biographers, claimed that the President's friends ' letters said he was "the most depressed person they've ever seen." He was overwhelmed by so much sadness that he had collapsed at least once. He showed strong signs, of severe depression, meaning that both his mother and many other members of his father's family suffered the same as he was likely genetically susceptible to illness. Lincoln was therefore, considered to be melancholic, a disorder that would be characterized by current mental health professionals as clinical depression. Whether he suffered from depression as a genetic preference or as a reaction to a combination of multiple emotional traumas in his life is the subject of the current debate. Lincoln, however, is an admirable character. Although he did not have access to formal education, he was able to achieve what some of the well-trained could not do. In all his hard work, he was a lawyer, a senator, and a member of the House of Representatives. He didn't blame anyone else for the lack of educational opportunities. Lincoln's leadership has brought massive change to the US. He changed the law and the constitution, in order to pave the way for a new America, one without slaves.

Although he was confronted, with a great deal of resistance, he still forced his policies across. Lincoln was a man, whose fame was filled with extreme poverty. He had four sons, three of whom died. Abraham Lincoln was assassinated in April 1865. The assailant burst into the President's private theater box and shot Lincoln in the back of his head. President Lincoln's successes have secured his eternal legacy. The Union was saved and the slaves were liberated. In his Gettysburg Address, he defined the civil war as a new commitment to the ideals set out in the Declaration of Independence.

Adolf Hitler

(1889 - 1945) Leader of Germany from 1934 to 1945

Adolf Hitler, leader of the Nazi party in Germany, was one of the most powerful and successful dictators of the 20th century. In order to gain absolute power, in Germany, Hitler capitalized on economic woes, public discontent and political infighting. The Third Reich, was born, on January 30, 1933, or, as the Nazis called it, the "Thousand Year Reich" (following Hitler's declaration that it would last for a millennium). The Nazi party, abbreviated by the "National Socialist German Workers" Party or the NSDAP, was a far-right political party in Germany that was active between 1920 and 1945.

It created and supported the ideology of National Socialism. Germany, when it was ruled by the Nazis, also called itself socialist, and although the government was a totalitarian government that dictated many things about the private lives of its citizens. The economy was still largely capitalistic and not entirely free, as there was state protectionism, sanctions and embargoes. While instigating World War II and the Holocaust, Adolf Hitler and his Nazi party committed one of the most heinous acts in history, causing tens of millions of lives to be lost and damaged beyond repair. Adolf Hitler, is often referred to as a madman and the most evil man ever to exist, partly because most people are unwilling to regard his person as anything other than a by-product of madness capable of such immensity of evil. But Hitler's, level of madness, has been the object of discord among historians, and how much of the evil he has committed can be attributed to illness, whether physically or mentally, remains the focus of debate. While Hitler had several psychiatric symptoms, i.e. extreme paranoia and dark behaviors, these issues added vast amounts of data to numerous textbooks on psychology, he was not really mentally ill in a clinical sense, according to modern historical account research.

Hitler's illusionary and paradoxical beliefs may be seen as a symptom of mental disorder, although most of his character was more than satisfactory.

The plethora of Hitler's physical illnesses is long. He had extreme stomach spasms, belching, bloating, and constipation. Beginning in the 1930s, he suffered from ringing and buzzing in his ears, hypertension, nausea and heart problems. He also had trouble with his vision after suffering two occurrences of blindness following a mustard gas injury in the First World War. Since the U.S. Government Office of Strategic Services commissioned Hitler's psychological profile to find new ways to fight him, psychoanalysis has been a common practice in trying to understand his personality. After Hitler's death, efforts were made to clarify his actions in psychological terms. Obviously, there are ample signs of the peculiarities of Hitler later in his life, of his sexual aversion, of his phobia, of his violent rage, of his paranoia, and of his own certainty that his death would have occurred in his early days. Hitler married Eva Braun in a bunker in Berlin at midnight on the night of April 28-29. After his personal will had been determined, Hitler shot himself in his suite on 30 April. According to Hitler's orders, their bodies were burned. Within days of his death, Berlin fell to the Soviets.

Agatha Christie

(1890 - 1976) Mystery and detective writer

The British novelist and playwright Agatha Christie, is credited with over 80 detective novels. Listed in the Guinness Book of Records as the "best-selling novelist" of all time, Agatha Christie worked tirelessly to sculpt stories and tactically astute characters that have astounded readers for decades. Christie's dedication to the ideal plot, nicknamed Queen of Crime, and earned her a place in literary history. Her writing style is only found among some of the best-selling writers like William Shakespeare.

According to UNESCO, Agatha Christie is the most widely translated author of all time and can be read in more than 103 different languages. Christie is reported to have suffered from bipolar disorder, contributing to her mysterious and famous disappearance. Two doctors, also diagnosed her with amnesia, which is a mental illness. Some experts believe that she also had a nervous breakdown due to her severe anxiety and depression. Her mother's death and her husband's infidelity are said to have caused her depression that year. In a hotel and under another guest name, Christie was discovered eleven days later after she had disappeared. She never spoke publicly about what happened to her. Agatha simply couldn't remember at the time what had happened to her. Despite numerous speculations, by the police, the press, and members of Agatha's family, we're probably never going to know what happened to her. Many of her books, have been adapted to movies, and many others have been tailored to radio, TV, comics and video games. In 1971, the Lady of Queen Elizabeth II was presented to Agatha for her services in literature. As Agatha Christie wrote her last books, scientists believe she might have been suffering from Alzheimer's disease. By the end of her life, her vocabulary had dropped from 15 to 30 percent, and according to a literature review, she had begun to repeat more phrases in her novels.

While memory loss and decreased vocabulary are often due to old age, all patients with Alzheimer's disease are known to have signs of memory failure. Agatha's health, began to decline in the 1970s, when she died in her home in Oxfordshire on 12 January 1976 due to natural causes. As a playwrighter, she is the only crime writer with an international reputation. In fact, her work today, is as famous and interesting as it has ever been. In 1972, Christie, was immortalized in wax for Madame Tussauds.

Albert Einstein

(1879 - 1955) Physicist and developer of the theory of relativity

At the beginning of the 20th century, Einstein broadened the human understanding of reality across all possible observational frames, from the smallest to the largest things in all of the known universe. Einstein questioned the concept of wave theory of light, and suggested, that light could also be seen as a collection of particles. It has led to a whole new view of reality, namely the theory of quantum mechanics. He was awarded the 1921 Nobel Prize for his theories.

At the beginning of his research, Einstein recognized Newton's mechanical weaknesses, and his theory of special relativity emerged from an attempt to describe the mechanical laws of nature in conjecture with the laws of the electromagnetic field that had been discovered. Einstein argued that a theory of gravity had to be properly interpreted throughout his work on the special theory of relativity, later he published his paper on the general theory of relativity in 1916. That theory, established the equivalence between mass and energy, leading to the famous formula $E = m c^2$. Einstein's peculiarities, were rich and complex. He grew slowly as a child and had a hard time learning to speak. He himself felt that his slow development as a child allowed him to think about the larger questions in life, the ones that contributed to his greatest discoveries. Einstein's primary school teachers confirmed that as a child he had an intense and annoying displeasure with the authorities, and he was often known for throwing tantrums. In addition, to his delayed ability to talk, some medical professionals suggested that this deviance might be seen as either symptomatic of autism or Asperger's syndrome. His habits, became even more strange as he grew older. He allowed his hair to grow long just to resist barbers, and he didn't wear socks because he thought they weren't necessary.

For all his great genius, Einstein relied heavily on smoking, not because of his genius, as some writers argue, but as a series of repeated actions to ease and comfort his daily routine. It was an acceptable balance, for Einstein's health and, inevitably, the path to his death. Einstein, had remarkable weak points and limitations which, in fact, seemed to place him clearly on the autism continuum spectrum. Later his abdominal aortic aneurysm burst, causing internal bleeding and severe pain. He traveled to Princeton University, but refused any further medical attention. He said, "When I want to go, I want to go. It's tasteless to prolong life artificially; I've done my share, it's time to go." Early in the morning of April 18, 1955, the doctor heard him say a few words in German that she couldn't understand, and then Einstein died.

Alan Turing

Alan Turing was a revolutionary pioneer in computer science. He is the founder of theoretical computers and of artificial intelligence. Turing is widely considered to have been at the forefront of our technological advances. Turing played a crucial role in cracking down on Nazi coded messages, enabling the Allies to overthrow the Nazis in a number of vital combat engagements, including the Battle of the Atlantic, and thus helped to win the war. Due to the problems of contrafactual history, it is difficult to determine the effect of Ultra Intelligence on the war effort.

But it is estimated at the top end that this work in Europe shortened the war by more than two years and saved a total of 14 million lives. Turing was extremely important in the development of theoretical computer science and provided a formalism for the computing theory of an algorithm with the creation of a Turing machine, which is seen as a model for a computer with a general purpose. It is not well known, but modern analysis shows that Turing had Asperger's Syndrome as it seemed quite obvious about social issues and the feelings of others, that he was unable to express his emotions, seek help or even tell the difference between a joke and a serious voice. One can say that Alan Turing, especially at that time, was not what society would define as normal. Because of his peculiar social behavior, he was not in very good form of mind: he was bullied at school and misinterpreted, isolated and despised by many in his adult life. Alan Turing was convicted and forced to choose between the custodian's sentence and chemical castration by hormonal injections after being prosecuted for admitting "homosexual acts" at the beginning of 1952. According to literature, at that time, the use of estrogen injections was intended to address "abnormal, uncontrolled" sexual drives. He chose this option in order to stay out of jail and continue his work despite the fact that his security clearance had been revoked.

As such his cryptographic mission could not be continued. Turing had some horrifying side effects from hormonal therapy, including impotence. Some of the reported side effects included breast swelling, mood changes and increased overall feminization. His medication, was withdrawn, in April 1953 and the University of Manchester established a five-year readership position for him; his suicide on 7 June 1954 caused a shock in the community.

Alexander the Great

(356 - 323 BC) King of Macedonia

Alexander, who was born a prince, had many advantages, as Aristotle himself taught him as a young boy. Instead of simply surpassing the deeds of his father, the King, he set out to surpass the deeds of mythical figures like Hercules. He was bold, both literally and figuratively, in leading his armies. Alexander's vision, his intelligence, his military genius, his charisma, his physical bravery and his leadership skills, are not up for debate. Over the course, of ten years, the men willingly followed him in battle and endured every possible deprivation.

The Greeks were united, the Persian Empire was defeated, and new territories from Greece to Egypt, Pakistan, and modern India were invaded. Alexander's great heritage, is represented, by the cultural distribution and mix of religions produced by his conquests, such as Greek Buddhism. In Egypt, he founded, 20 cities, most notably Alexandria, which bore his name. Military historians, class him as one of the greatest general tactics ever experienced. The Iliad «Troy's story» was with him in all his campaigns being his favorite book. His mother kept telling him stories as a child, and he believed that he was equal, if not superior, to Achilles, who was essentially the current superman of the time. The latter biographers, spent considerable time, describing the conflicting character elements of Alexander, the philosopher and butcher, the dreamer and tyrant, the charming and friendly, but also someone who stabbed his friends in the back. Incoherence, in the character, of the warlord was acknowledged by references to his complex relationship with his dead father, Philip II, or to his megalomania after becoming the world's leading ruler. As the ancient hero Achilles, was famous, Alexander took a strong position in Greek and non-Greek mythology and legendary traditions. It has become the benchmark against which military leaders have been measured, military academies around the world continue to teach his tactics.

He is one of the most influential people in history. As Alexander the Great, died in Babylon in 323 B.C., his body, according to historical accounts, did not begin to show signs of decay until after the first six days of his death. It confirmed to the ancient Greeks what they all believed which was that Alexander the Macedonian King was no ordinary man, but a god.

Aldous Huxley

(1894-1963) Writer and philosopher

Aldous Huxley's popular revival, more than a century after his birth, and more than 80 years since his best-known novel Brave New World was published, points out that his thoughts are as relevant today as they were in his time. The book was an immense achievement. His prediction of a society that has been made convenient by the consumption of goods, never-ending amusements, the false possibility of change, and the artificial well-being of American sentiment remain valid until today. Compared to other influential authors from the early twentieth century, such as George Orwell.

Huxley's unusual identification and exploration of philosophical themes revealed social fault lines separating our rationalist interests from the perceptual needs of all. While Huxley also described the adverse effects of psychedelic drugs in the "Brave New World", he was nevertheless active in mescaline research and praised mescaline and LSD in "The Doors of Perception" as physically benign, potentially therapeutic and spiritually enlightening. In 1967, during the Summer of Love, "psychedelic" would soon become the preferred term for the sensation triggered by mescaline and LSD. Early life was difficult for Huxley. His mother died of cancer during his childhood, his brother committed suicide, and he began to have vision problems. His cornea suffered a condition called "keratitis" which was swollen after infection and he could a such not see well. After being close to loss of his vision, it recovered enough so he was able to read and study with a lens. Huxley, also wrote in Hindu and Buddhist terms, about spiritual ideas, pacifism, harmony, and mysticism. The rest of his life's work was embodied in the concepts of meditation, enlightenment, self-realization, and many other transcendental ideals of Eastern philosophy. He renounced all forms of war, this ultimately prevented him from becoming a citizen of the United States due to his pacifist views.

Huxley richly expressed his views on the risks of global overpopulation. He warned that a dysfunctional society and economy would lead to a more powerful government and social instability, a view which shows that overpopulation would lead to a loss of food security and fewer resources to be used per person. Huxley's thinking, is a precursor, to today's concepts of sustainable living and production, environmentalism and the ideals of cooperative life. His reflections on Eastern thinking, ecology, non-hierarchical societies, and psychedelic drugs have made him a prominent counter-culture man whose political impact still largely defines today's political environment. Huxley died on 22 November 1963 after being diagnosed with larynx cancer three years earlier.

Andreas Vesalius

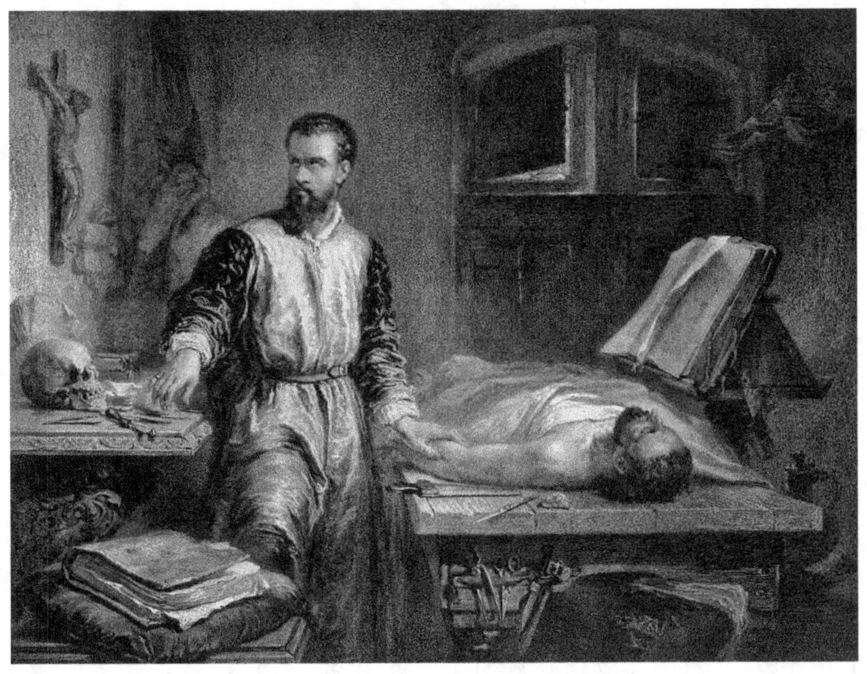

Andreas Vesalius learned the arts and Latin, common at the time, he also learned Greek and Hebrew, too. He received his degree, in Arts in 1532 and was admitted to the prestigious medical school of the University of Paris. A major anatomist and founder of modern medical science, Vesalius is known for his knowledge which was not based on traditions, but on facts. He indeed had, a very tumultuous life. He was expelled from the University of Louvain, Belgium, as a student.

He searched for temporary shelter in Paris but finally got his place in Padua, Italy. They allowed him to take final examinations almost immediately, as such Vesalius was awarded his doctorate just before his 23rd birthday. Vesalius was quickly appointed professor of anatomy and operation at the university by senior academics. In 1543 «De humini corporus fabrica» was published, his remarkable book was a complete illustrated work of anatomy of the human body. The book overthrew myths of anatomy lasting over a thousand years, his findings were based on his observations made during dissections. He was also appointed, as a court physician in Spain, making his reputation known throughout the world. As Vesalius dissected the body of a Spanish nobleman who died in his care, he learned that the heart still beats after death for a short time. As a result, he was suspected of murder, and taken before the Inquisition. The death penalty of Vesalius was commuted to a pilgrimage to the Holy Land ordered by the King. The mystery is why, during this period, he actually decided to make his journey to the Holy Land, as it was common in those days as a penance for a sinful act. His journey, was hindered by violent storms upon his return from Jerusalem. Vesalius got sick when his ship entered the port on the Greek island of Zakynthos. He died, in the course of a few days.

There have been no official records found
regarding his death on the rural island, and no one
has yet been able to find his burial site. All of history,
is characterized by brilliant people whose scientific
discoveries have transformed our medical practice
and our understanding of the biological phenomena of
the human body, both in health and in the state of
illness. One of these geniuses is Andreas Vesalius.

Aristotle

(384 - 322 BC) Philosopher

Aristotle made contributions to logic, metaphysics, mathematics, biology, botany, ethics, law, agriculture, chemistry, medicine and theatre. He is a prominent figure of ancient Greek philosophy. He was a student of Plato who was studying under Socrates. Aristotle was empirically more focused, than either Plato or Socrates, and he was well known for opposing Plato's theory of forms. Aristotle transformed most, if not all, of the fields of knowledge he touched as a prolific writer and polymath.

It is not shocking that the philosopher Thomas Aquinas referred to him as "The Philosopher." Aristotle, wrote almost, 200 treatises in his lifetime, of which only 31 survive to this day. Unfortunately, these works are not intended for general readers, as they are in the form of lecture notes or draft manuscripts, so that the work does not reveal its renowned prose richness, which has attracted many great adherents, including Roman Cicero. Aristotle was the first to separate human knowledge areas into different fields, including mathematics, biology and ethics. These are still some of the most well-known classifications used today. As the originator of the field of logic, he was also the first to develop a formal system of reasoning. Aristotle found that the structure could decide the truth of any statement, rather than the substance. His syllogism is a classic example of a valid argument: "All men are mortals; Socrates is a man; therefore Socrates is a mortal man." In view of the structure of this statement, the claim is assumed to be true as long as the premises are valid. 2000 years later, the modern idea, of propositional logic has risen above the philosophy of Aristotle, which once dominated this field of thought. Aristotle, as opposed to Plato, was more concerned about what is real in the world, his realism is about what we see and what we can touch.

He believed that human beings do not want to transcend human self-centeredness, as it is a prominent part of who we are as creatures. That is why, Aristotle, wanted to design a government and a society that recognizes human egotism and seeks to mitigate our indifferences through communication. His goal for the human race, was to create a working government while recognizing human egotism. Not the ideal state as Plato had imagined, but rather a state that functions. He referred to this as "Polis", the "political community," which would be a balanced state that upholds private property and the structure of the family, but gives both rich and poor, a chance to work together for the common good. Aristotle also thought that the heart was important to the mind's intelligence, not just the brain. In his thesis, he wrote the initial principles of the learning, of thought and reasoning, which would determine the direction of the history of modern psychology. Many of his ideas continue to influence our methods of today; it is the first known text in the psychological literature, "About the Mind," named "Para Psyche." Aristotle's work is based on the work of the early philosophers and their studies. Since many of the early Greek studies have been written down, they have provided the basis for thinking in modern mental health settings.

After the death, of Alexander the Great, Aristotle was at the time considered a Macedonian sympathizer and, therefore, convicted and sentenced to death. In 322, he rather died of a gastrointestinal issue a little north of the town of Chalcis.

Arthur Schopenhauer

(1788 - 1860) Philosopher

One of the greatest philosophers of the 19th century, Schopenhauer seems to have had more influence on academic philosophy and literature than on the general population. The pessimist stance, and psychology of the will, are known as the hallmark teachings of Schopenhauer. He predicted some aspects of cognitive neuroscience, psychoanalysis, and evolutionary psychology, but most modern practitioners do not easily identify with his efforts. Schopenhauer, taught his philosophy to Nietzsche.

Nietzche was very excited, about his relationship with the composer Richard Wagner, because their friendship, was based on their mutual discovery of Schopenhauer.

In fact, Nietzsche's «Will-to-Power» work is a rewriting of Schopenhauer's "Will to Live." Thanks to the influence, of his aesthetics, on later generations of artists from all walks of life, Arthur Schopenhauer was dubbed the philosopher of the artist. He is widely known as the philosopher of pessimism as he articulates an absolute perspective that questions the meaning and value of life and its existence. He considered the truth about reality to be guided by a blind will, which in humans expresses itself as illogical and futile desires. It was, a kind of asceticism to him, one, that could willingly make us give up a lot of our material comfort in the fight against this unreasonable will. Schopenhauer came from a wealthy family, and because he had enough money to live as a young man he didn't need to work. Compared to the agony and cruelty of his philosophy, even by modern standards, he most certainly had a very decent life. The work of philosophers rarely represents their experience of life, not any more than that of the life of scientists, because of its abstract nature, philosophy is far from having an impact on everyday life.

As a rare thing, being between a philosopher and a fanatical pessimist, Schopenhauer does not promise consolation in history: man's lot is meant to be wretched, regardless of how politically stable he is when alive under any given structure of society.

Schopenhauer was also strongly influenced by the understanding of Hindu and Buddhist philosophies. The world as being everything we can and do know, is in fact an illusion, this is one of the most important ideas of Buddhism. In other words, only through our own experiences can we know the world that ultimately hides the truth about reality from us. Siddhartha Gautama, the Buddha, was responsible for these philosophical views that he held. Schopenhauer may have had some underlying vulnerability to depression evident in his pessimism, this may also have arisen or increased as a result of various stressful life events. On September 21, 1860, while sitting on his couch at home, he died, the cause of which was presumed to be pulmonary-respiratory failure.

Athanasius Kircher

(1602 - 1680) Jesuit scholar

Athanasius Kircher, also known as the "Master of Hundred Arts," was a polymath who mastered everything from anatomy to medicine and religion. Yet Kircher didn't just study all of these things, he also seems to have believed in everything. In an age of growing mythological skepticism by scientists such as René Descartes, Kircher strongly believed in the nature of mythical beasts and beings such as sirens, giants, dragons, basilisks and angels.

Coming from war-torn Germany as a refugee, at the time of Galileo's arrest, Kircher arrived in Rome where he was known for his know-how of the secrets of deciphering hieroglyphs. He published more than thirty works on topics ranging from optics to art, Egyptology, magnetism and music. Kircher was one of the most popular scholars in the world during much of his scientific career. He achieved his significance in two ways: by adding to science with information from his correspondence with more than 760 other scientists and physicists, and in particular by communicating with his Jesuit brothers, he also added much clarity to his own research and experiments. His works, are a combination, of legitimate research results, sophisticated partnerships, forward-looking insights, mere speculation and impressive advertising from today's perspective. Certainly, the man's enthusiasm for scientific research and his never-ending curiosity about the workings of the world which cannot be denied. While he tended towards the sick during the bubonic plague in Roma in 1656, he still took time to study microorganisms with a microscope in order to find a cure. A cure was not identified, but his investigations followed a germ disease hypothesis that was well ahead of his day's scientific orthodoxy.

He avoided death many times, starting with an injury to his leg when he was a young boy that had turned gangrene which according to him, the Virgin Mary had miraculously healed when she visited one of her sanctuaries. On his way to Austria, he was shipwrecked on an island and was almost hanged on another of his many trips by overly enthusiastic Protestant cavalrymen. He traveled to southern Italy, Sicily and Malta for his last great adventure and experienced two volcanoes erupting and even attempted descending into the active crater of Vesuvius. Upon his death, in 1680, and even until the end of the 20th century, Kircher's work was generally oppressed by disrespect. However, from that moment on, a certain revival took place.

Baruch Spinoza

In the early modern era, Spinoza, along with Descartes and Leibniz, was seen as one of the most influential rationalist philosophers. Also, in this same period, Spinoza became Europe's most prominent "atheist." Though often persecuted as an atheist in his own time, Spinoza's writings became a key part of the shaping of philosophy, theology and politics in the centuries to come. "Atheist" meant someone, at that time, who had denied the conventional biblical concepts of God and his connection to the natural world. Throughout Spinoza's approach, the mind was born entirely in the natural environment of the body, and the two created human consciousness of the self.

Spinoza called for a radical new understanding of the universe to surpass the standard Judeo-Christian beliefs, his views, were introduced in his most important book entitled "Ethics Demonstrated in a Geometrical Manner." He claims that there is no transcendent and personal God, no eternal soul, no free will, and thus the universe does not exist for any ultimate purpose or reason. Using a geometric method to create his theory, it was similar to the work of Euclid Elements, and later Newton's Principia. Alternatively, Spinoza suggests that everything that happens in the natural world, including human beings, could not have happened any differently, so that the world follows one and the same set of laws of nature in which human beings are by no means unique. Spinoza also denied the immortality of the soul; he firmly denies that the God of Abraham, Isaac, and Jacob is a transcendent providential God; and he argues that God has not given the law, or that it is literally binding upon the Jews. As a European Jew, in the 17th century, who denied the infallibility of the Bible, young Spinoza was condemned by both the powerful organized Church and the rabbinical clergy. Spinoza could have been executed if he had lived somewhere less acceptable than in the relatively tolerant city of Amsterdam. Everything is one: the notion of Spinoza that everything is God, and the universe, like the human self, is one and the same.

Based on a growing demographic that sees itself as spiritual but not religious. Spinoza's point of view, appeals to those, who do not believe in an anthropomorphic god but are not happy with a universe devoid of order and unity. Spinoza died, when he fell ill in 1677. It's not exactly clear what caused his death. Speaking as one of the most visible and persuasive advocates of freedom of speech, democracy and the integrity of philosophical life, his philosophy has always been a milestone for the democratic constituent of modern culture.

Bertrand Russell

In 1950, the British philosopher, mathematician and writer Bertrand Russell was awarded the Nobel Prize in Literature. At first, he may not appear, to be a man who has, the secret to happiness. In fact, he lived a great deal of his life between either experiencing abundance or scarcity. When he was only six years old, this controversial thinker was struck by the grief of losing his family. After that, he stayed with his strict grandparents. From a very young age, he felt that life was almost unbearable. Later, he admitted that he was thinking of suicide on more than one occasion.

Russell supported his children and grandchildren with a home and education, and he fought for their sakes to save his marriages. He endured, immensely, against the destructive actions of his second and third wife. As he loved his children dearly, he was completely devastated by the time his son John was afflicted with schizophrenia. Russell's life was filled with the kind of occurrences that make up the lives of many others, mainly because he lived for a very long time, but also because he had an enormous amount of emotional and mental strength. He was married four times, published an incredibly large number of important intellectual books and articles on philosophy, and repeatedly faced problems with the law in relation to his anti-war sentiment. He was also refused admission to the City University of New York because the court ruled that Russell was "morally unfit" to teach at American universities because of the opinions he found in his book «Marriage and Morals.» After the First World War, Russell began his third career, writing as a freelance journalist and pamphleteer on politics and ethics. Russell, often changed his mind, on political issues, without even recognizing it to others around him. In the decades that followed, Russell flooded global leaders with telegrams calling for peace and disarmament as the threat of nuclear war increased.

Russell's advocacy for a world government was underpinned by the profound displeasure of humanity. He was convinced that human beings could not manage conflicts in a civilized way, and that peace could only be achieved by force. Russel died, in his own home in Wales. He was just 97 years old. There is still plenty of justification for paying attention to Bertrand Russell's life and legacy many decades after his death. Not only because he was one of the pioneers of analytical philosophy, but also because he was a highly skilled academic, public intellectual, critical of organized religion, humanist, and one of the most prominent peace activists during the twentieth century.

King Charles VI

(1368 - 1422) French king

The world seemed to fall apart when Charles VI was born, most of the horrors that we now compare to the Middle Ages, such as intellectual ignorance, plagues, famine, poverty, rural robbers, and constant war trends, date back to this period of time. Charles VI as an adult became a hero, while as a child, a medieval prince would have been able to expect the best education. When his father died, Charles, then 11 years old, became King. The regency was shared by his four uncles. Six years have passed before Charles overthrowing of his uncles, his actions have been as just as they emptied the treasury. By 1386, Charles had restored his father's counselors, and forced his uncles away from Paris.

Charles began to rise to the greatness that France had demanded of him in order to face the English threat. When Charles grew up, he never showed signs of mental or emotional distress, but current knowledge tells us that schizophrenia usually develops for the first time in adolescents and in the early twenties of young people. At the age of 23, in 1392, Charles went on a hunting trip with his entourage, apparently at that moment he went completely berserk. Suddenly, he stabbed one of his knights and killed him on the spot as he grabbed the sword and threw himself at the rest of the group of hunters. The king, managed to kill three other knights, before he could be stopped. In 1393, a year after the journey, Charles seemed to forget his own name, and he did not recognize his own wife when she was brought to him. Compared to republics, with a general consensus in principle, absolute monarchies, are authorized by God, and you are not entitled to vote on any matter of governance. The authority, is therefore, accepted by the people, because God never makes mistakes. There was no democratic system in medieval France, and therefore Charles the Mad, the newly baptized King, was allowed to continue on the throne. In 1405 Charles VI refused to wash himself and threatened to kill those who had approached and touched him according to Pope Pius II.

Charles VI, once known as Charles the Beloved, and later Charles the Mad, died in 1422, at the age of 61, probably of natural causes. Two of his descendants, were crowned, to succeed him because of the general uncertainty prevailing in the nation. At that time, Joan of Arc was ten years old, and after all, France finally got a true hero.

Charles Darwin

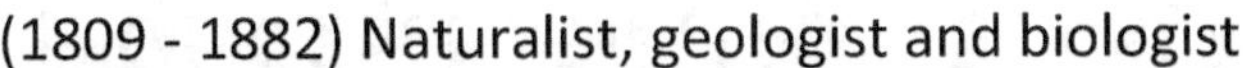

(1809 - 1882) Naturalist, geologist and biologist

Of course, the theory of evolution is the creation of Charles Darwin. He traveled the world, saw all kinds of life, and finally wrote a revolutionary book on the origins of the species through which he forever changed our scientific knowledge of our nature. This suggested that all animals in the world originated from common ancestors and through a natural selection cycle, evolve, grow and sometimes become extinct, a process that has been taking place since the beginning of life.

Some biographers believe that Charles Darwin came to his great idea of the origin of the species when he was a very young man about thirty years old. However, for another 21 years, he did not publish his thesis. It is marvelous that he waited so long, Darwin's perspective was fascinating, knowing that he could not afford to allow his analysis and his theory to fall under the control of others, or to be disqualified by others because of his Christian faith. Darwin managed to remain true to his ability to navigate creation with confidence, while still allowing the possibility for his theory to coexist as a science alongside his religious convictions. Scholars, are also debating, what Darwin's challenges were, but whatever they were, they were substantial. After five years of successful trips, Darwin was practically permanently disabled. Although he endured the physical symptoms and causes of all his illness, they appeared to be largely related to a serious case of agoraphobia, which kept him virtually bedridden and in constant shaking, hysteric mood swings, vomiting and long-lasting visual hallucination since he was 30 years old. Fear of people meant that Darwin even avoided interactions with his own children. In one letter, he articulated his feelings of suicide because of the publication of his work, which caused much controversy, this left him deeply depressed by the origin of the species.

Signs of recurring OCD and hypochondria may have been visible to others in his personality, all of his new and repeated symptoms have been extensively documented by himself. There are many, interesting points, to be found in the analysis of his death. The celebrated naturalist, better known for his technical theory of evolution and natural selection, died on 19 April 1882 after suffering a series of heart attacks in the last few years. At that time, the wisdom, intuition and motivation needed to formulate and understand such a theory that he created must have been very difficult. It has remained constant for over 200 years, much thanks to the increasing amount of later scientific evidence proving its key statements.

Charles Dickens

(1812 - 1870) Writer and social critic

Dickens was prominent during the Romantic and Victorian eras, as an English novelist he was considered as one of the English language's most popular writers. His creations have remained in the public consciousness thanks to the vibrant personality of the characters, suspense of drama and moral wisdom. It seems that his writing was not the only kind of excellence that Dickens strived to achieve in his life. Dickens developed from hopeless poverty into a "self-made man," being among the first of authors that managed to be fully supportive of himself through his art successfully.

His immaculate observations of human nature were not only exceptional, it was also remarkable that his stories, books, and other writings were created very rapidly. Reports indicate the author despised if a single strand of hair was out of place and would comb his hair obsessively all day long. He usually, would dictate, his thoughts and writing to an assistant and pass over the same sentences repeatedly, this may have been a form of compulsive obsessive disorder, which experts have suspected that he suffered of. Dickens became the world's most popular writer at the end of his 30s. He was rich and his life seemed to be in harmony. But Dickens would begin to fall down into depressions with the beginning of each new novel, his condition was probably caused by an incredibly difficult childhood, which saw the author working in a boot factory and live on his own when his father was put in jail. Dickens friends said that each time he started working on a new idea his mood would slowly increase, but by the time that the project was finished he was in a form of mania. With aging he got worse, he eventually moved in together with an eighteen-year-old actress when he separated from his wife, the mother of his 10 children. When he experienced a train crash just four years before his death, he was lucky to be unhurt although he was forced to assist dying passengers before help arrived.

After the accident, his anxiety ultimately seemed to have hindered his imagination, and his formerly prolific success almost ended as well. He became one of the most politically revolutionary figures in his time, as many writers, philosophers and even political leaders, he also mentioned the injustices and immoralities seen during his time, they were in his mind a sign of the world being corrupted by industrial power. He portrayed, his challenging views, in his works as a warning sign to new generations of readers. Dickens died, after a stroke, on the 9th of June 1870, in England, he was 58 years old. With his lasting attributes of sympathy, belief, compassion and empathy with humanity, he remains one of the world's most loved authors.

David Bohm

(1917–1992) Theoretical physicist

David Bohm's greatest achievement in science is his understanding of the essence of physical reality, which focuses on his theoretical research, particularly that of quantum theory. Bohm argued that every component of the universe consists of information about the physical reality as a whole. Therefore, each part of the universe "contains" the entire universe in some way. In 1952, Bohm claimed that the particles were really particles, not only when they were observed. His theory is based on the force he called the "pilot wave," which is affected by the action of the observers, and therefore every attempt to detect a particle also alters its behavior.

The interpretation of Bohm eliminates the quantum paradox of the wave-particle duality but preserves and even emphasizes the ability of one particle to instantly affect another over long distance through non-locality. Bohm suggested that these invisible or hidden variables of subquantum forces and particles, can in fact explain the strange behavior of subatomic particles. Thus, the apparent oddity could occur through hidden means, which, in turn, do not conflict with common ideas of causality and the construction of reality. Thinkers like Newton and Descartes, during the Enlightenment period, replaced the old natural concept of a universal order based on the mechanistic interpretation. Bohm was popular for his sensible understanding of quantum mechanics even after the emergence of Einstein's relativity and theory of quantum mechanics He saw the cosmos as infinite and unknowable; he thus created a vision of an endless array of looping hierarchies, all of which constituted an implied hidden order. Bohm believed, that science, could not fully describe the universe and, as such, solidified his spirituality and established his ontological theories. He also assumed that the brain, at a cellular level, functions according to the mathematics of certain quantum effects and that thinking itself, is also simply a quantum occurrence of distributed and non-localized effects.

Bohm made a wide and diversified positive difference to physics, but not without dispute. He was, a philosopher-scientist, one who, like the ancients, belonged to the old school category of thinkers. The primary theory of Bohm is that all reality is a dynamic process. This process includes the method of thinking itself and learning about the nature of existence. The awareness of physical reality in Bohm's mind completely transforms the common idea of "empty space." To Bohm, space is not the vast vacuum in which matter passes; space is all the more real as the object moves within it. Thus, space and matter, are inextricably linked. Indeed, modern calculations of the amount known as «zero-point energy» show that one cubic centimeter of empty space actually contains more energy than all matter in the entire universe. In 1949, because of his Marxist opinions, and Communist affiliations, Bohm was subjected to a federal government investigation and forced to leave the United States. His academic work continued in other countries, but he had a hard time away from home without any friends or colleagues nearby as he was prone to depression. After a heart attack, on 27 October 1992, Bohm died, at the age of 74 in London.

David Bowie

(1947–2016) Singer

David Bowie was an English rock star, known for Ziggy Stardust being one of his dramatic musical transformations. He spent five decades, building his career, and is considered an emblematic figure in modern pop music. Bowie's work, also dealt, with personal inner realities and existential dilemmas. His sound and his look have always been transforming. He toured the United States where he became very popular, his unique look was only to some extent similar to that of Queen Freddie Mercury.

They shared a unique sexual ambiguity and androgyny which fitted well into the growing radicalization and culture of sexual awakening in the late 1960s and 1970s. He was afraid of being diagnosed with schizophrenia, as were two of his aunts, the third being confined to a mental asylum. His half-brother, Terry, was also diagnosed with schizophrenia and reportedly had distinct periods of psychosis as he became one of Bowie's most influential early personality models. Indeed, David was very afraid that his mind would also succumb to schizophrenia later in his life. David took an interest in music at an early age and began to play saxophone when he was 13. His brother Terry, nine years older, introduced young David to the worlds of rock music, and he inspired him greatly. The tragedy became the focal point of the later Bowie track, "Jump They Say", it was the result of Terry who committed suicide in 1985. Another song by David, «The Madmen», vividly portrayed madness and the treatment of people suffering from asylum. A few years later, Bowie himself was presumed to have had a psychotic episode, which he himself attributed mainly to the period when he took very large amounts of cocaine. In a tribute to the notoriously idiosyncratic performer, a recurring theme emerged after his death: his relevance to those who felt that they were misfits in society.

The LGBT community and many others resonated with Bowie's androgyny, his theatrical showmanship, and his ability to redefine himself. Bowie has offered positive representation to many, which was extremely lacking in his time and is still very rare today. Bowie's constructive gestures of non-compliance have inspired many people. Ziggy Stardust, a bisexual, alien alter ego, described androgyny and nonheterosexuality as something beautiful and worthy of celebration. The music icon passed away on January 10, 2016, two days after its 69th birthday. Bowie has created a remarkable musical heritage of 26 albums.

Diana, Princess of Wales

(1961 - 1997) Member of the British royal family

After her father inherited the title Earl Spencer, Princess Diana became Lady Diana Spencer in 1975. She married Prince Charles, the current heir to the British throne, on 29th of July 1981. Two sons, were born into marriage, before they divorced in 1996. Over the years, Diana had to deal with anxiety as the pair began to fall apart. Reports of infidelity on both sides were published in the media during their marriage. The "People's Princess" was open to communication and of support for her struggles during postnatal depression which are endured by many women.

Diana felt overwhelmed by her royal duties as the media coverage of almost every aspect of her life became unbearable after the couple's fairy tale wedding. During an interview, Princess Diana talked about how she had previously suffered from eating disorders. She said that everyone in her family knew about her condition, while everyone seemed to blame Prince Charles for it being a consequence of their marriage falling apart. Princess Diana was far more than a royal, a fashion icon and a caring mother, someone who yearned to help as many people as she possibly could. She is recognized as a true humanitarian. The "People's Princess" was always been eager to have a positive impact on people around the world, from raising awareness of HIV/AIDS, to promoting a ban on landmines. By virtue of, her own merit, Diana became an enormous international icon. For many years, her exquisite style has influenced fashion trends. Her contribution to charity won the respect and gratitude of the people. As the Egyptian filmmaker and playboy Dodi Fayed began to date her in 1997, Diana kicked the British tabloids in a frenzy unlike anything seen before. Diana and Dodi Fayed were both involved in a car crash during their trip to Paris and after trying to escape from the Paparazzi on 31 August 1997, Fayed and the driver both died on the scene and were declared dead.

Initially Diana survived the impact but died a few hours later due to her wounds in a hospital in Paris. She was at that time only thirty-six years old. After her death, the Princess of Wales Memorial Fund was set up to provide, among other things, palliative care, criminal reform and assisted asylum. The Fund continues to carry out its charitable efforts. The Fund was integrated into the Duke and Duchess of Cambridge and the Prince Harry Royal Foundation in 2013.

Edvard Munch

(1863 - 1944) Painter and printmaker

Well known as an expressionist and printer, Munch was a Norwegian-born artist. At the end of the 20th century, he played a major role in German expressionism and later art forms. This was, attributed, to the great mental suffering that many of the pieces he produced seem to show. He was related by blood to other famous artists; Jacob Munch (painter) and Peter Munch (historian). In 1868, Edvard Munch's mother died of tuberculosis just a few years after his birth after which he was raised by his father. Their dad raised them with irrational fears for deeper problems, this is part of why Edvard Munch's work took on a deeper tone, and why, as an artist, he is known to have been so emotionally oppressed.

In January of 1892, while in Oslo, he suffered what is known as the most famous panic attack in the world. Munch documented the incident in his diary: he was looking out over the fjord and clouds turned red blood and he felt a scream going through nature. Although it is not known if Munch had been extensively depressed, other members of his family had indeed been mentally unstable. In 1908, Munch was also affected by dire alcoholism, which made his suffering from a possible mental disorder worse. Eventually he was admitted to a mental health clinic in Denmark. In 1937, in addition to his known mental disorders, the artists saw his works confiscated by Hitler's government and considered to be "degenerate art." Neurasthenia, a psychiatric condition for paranoia and hypochondria, has been diagnosed on his conditions. His writings are characterized by people with a clear sense of grief and suffering through his paintings. Munch often showed his own feelings with avid strokes and deep colors. On 23 January 1944, at the age of 80 of cardiovascular disease. Edvard Munch's works, of art, are considered world heritage. In his will, he left the city of Oslo and its people with all his immense works of art. His works of art, are universally popular, because of their incredible portrait of the human condition.

Edward Teller

Teller was an American theoretical physicist who
was born in Hungary. Teller, studied nuclear and
molecular physics, spectroscopy and surface physics.
In the 20th century, he was the pioneer of the
hydrogen bomb and would become a much more
vilified scientist than any other before him, but his
critics were always rejected as being naive,
unpatriotic, and ignorant of what science really wants
to achieve. Yet Teller wasn't just a fan of nuclear
weapons.

He always valued the science of the bomb, as his plans showed that it could be used for many other purposes, beyond killing innocent people instantly. He dreamed of; nuclear machines, larger, smaller, stronger, subterranean, and aeronautical, and rocket fuel in orbit, on the moon, and more and more of them in a myriad of applications. Teller proposed the construction of an artificial deep-water port by means of an underwater hydrogen bomb, the extraction of oil by nuclear explosions, and the development of a second Panama Canal by nuclear power. Nevertheless, he acknowledged that his political motivation to claim nuclear weapons as the greatest deterrent was justifiable. Teller pointed out that his stand on such weapons was influenced by his first-hand experience of the politics of tyrannical rule. He lived under the Communists and the Fascists as they brought hell to Hungary before he finally emigrated to America in the 1930's. His scars were not only psychological in nature: Teller fell under a moving streetcar and lost his right foot, replaced by an artificial prosthetic when he studied at the University of Munich. He endured his handicap for the rest of his life and hobbled as he walked. Teller's strong support for nuclear weapons and nuclear power, especially when many of his wartime fellow workers later expressed regret at the arms race, made him a simple target for the stereotype of the "mad scientist."

He inspired Stanley Kubrick to create "Dr. Strangelove." Teller was not worried about his reputation as being the father of the hydrogen bomb, despite the fact that he felt the name was in a bad taste. At the end of the day, he insisted on not being morally responsible for his discoveries, a view he held together with many other scientists of his day. He received the Albert Einstein Award, the Enrico Fermi Award and the National Medal of Science in 1991 and was also awarded one of the first Ig Nobel Prizes in recognition of his "Lifelong efforts to change the meaning of peace as we know it." President George W. Bush awarded him the Presidential Medal of Freedom in less than two months before his death.

Elvis Presley

Elvis Presley had "a larger than life" lifestyle, from his humble origins in Tupelo, Mississippi, to his Rock & Roll stardom, and to his death in 1977 at the age of 42. And he wasn't without his eccentricities, like a lot of rock stars before him. He was, definitely, the most successful artist of the time. Rock' n' Roll had already become quite popular, and Elvis brought prominence to that genre when he came to the stage. Elvis never invented rock' n' roll, yet for many reasons he became known as the "King of Rock' n' Roll."

There is no question that the sound of rock was largely shaped by Elvis, and his energetic sex appeal and great talent only contributed to his popularity. Not only, did Elvis, turn the world of music completely on his head with his unique style of sound and powerful performances, but his music also had a major impact on other performers. The non-stop tour activity and Las Vegas commitment that he had, ultimately led to his physical and spiritual deterioration. All those, demanding routines, have been seen as contributing to his heavy dependence on a number of prescription drugs. In this regard, he, suffered greatly from his own success. He achieved his objectives so easily that he did not face any more challenges. After his mother Gladys died, he lost his physical bearings and began taking drugs on a routine basis. Elvis met Priscilla when she was fourteen years old and moved with him at the age of seventeen. They married when she was 22 years old and welcomed their first and only child the following year, at which point he lost his sexual interest in her and divorced her. Elvis's health problems, worsened, as he was depressed after they had divorced in 1973. Elvis seemed to be suffering from narcissism, depression, eating disorders, drug addiction, and possibly also a minor Christ complex, as clinical psychologists later claimed.

Elvis was a well-known womanizer, and everyone, including Priscilla, knew of his many adulterous affairs. His influence has never faded, and even decades after his death his popularity has steadily increased. Rumors that Elvis is still alive abound while his career in effect has never ended over the years. His music, continues, to sell well, every year thousands visit Graceland, and every corner of Vegas you can still see the Elvis impersonator. Not only, did Elvis change, the world dramatically when he was alive, but his legacy still lives on and his music still has an impact on our world and culture.

Ernest Hemingway

(1899 - 1961) Author and journalist

Ernest Hemingway was an American novelist and author of short stories, his work is characterized by minimalism and simplicity based on his vast experience during the First World War, the Spanish Civil War and the Second World War. Hemingway had a major impact on the development of fiction both in America and abroad in the 20th century. The writings of many other contemporary novelists and authors, and their image of the disillusioned anti-hero, draw many traces of his writing style.

Through his works, Hemingway tried to reconcile the tragedy of his time with a life-long faith of action through victory, success and grace. Hemingway, had major, paranoia problems, while on a number of occasions, his doctor prescribed electrotherapy without success in treating his crippling anxiety. He had a dubious reputation as a KGB collaborator. After the FBI unveiled its Hemingway file on the basis of a Freedom of Information petition, the files finally revealed that he had indeed been placed under federal surveillance. In 1935, during his time in the Bahamas, he began to use the non-conventional method of catching fish with a machine gun. He did so in order to avoid scavenging of his catch. This, aggressive technique, did not work so well because of the aggravation of predators, such as sharks, which severely attacked his catch. During his career, as a writer, he published seven novels, six collections of short stories and two non-fiction books. All of these were produced while he was standing in his bedroom in front of a bookcase, his favorite writing position. He could wear out seven pencils in his most productive days. Having survived; skin cancer, measles, hepatitis, diabetes and blood poisoning, and even two fatal plane crashes, his wife was understandably unwilling to believe that he had actually killed himself just before his 62nd birthday.

Hemingway has left behind a remarkable collection and iconic writing style, one that still influences many writers today. He was, a great personality, constantly seeking as great adventures as his creative abilities. Hemingway was celebrated for reviving the genre of short story style, and his use of declarative sentences are still applauded today.

Ernesto "Che" Guevara

(1928 – 1967) Marxist revolutionary

Ernesto Guevara's name has become synonymous with rebellion, revolution, and socialism, lamented by some, regretted by other. He was born to a middle-class family and did not suffer as many other children in Latin America did from poverty and hunger. He suffered, from ill health as a young boy however. His adventurous and honest rebellious mindset was in some ways linked to his early years suffering of serious asthma. Analysis of Ernesto "Che" Guevara's most famous biographies also suggests he may have had ADHD.

Supporters say he was a patriot who fought and died for his convictions and consider him a romantic symbol of the common goal of freedom through struggle. Some refer to the Cuban government's position as a proof of the injury caused by its dogmatic belief in socialism, which carried out extrajudicial killings and political repression. He eventually, traveled for a long stretch of time, this period, marked the beginning of a an extended odyssey that opened his eyes to the reality of the circumstances he existed within. His long journeys in Latin America would come to shape his political views and give him a genuine purpose over the years, namely that the solution to the widespread poverty and cruelty was communism through revolution. After briefly completing his medical studies at the University of Buenos Aires, Dr. Guevara left Argentina for a future in politics, one that would make him a part of the South American and African revolutions. Guevara is well known for his involvement in the Cuban Revolution. He together with Fidel Castro ousted the former head of state. He was a key figure in the revolution and was officially named minister of trade and president of Cuba's National Bank. and, In his new position, he flew around the earth, as the country's ambassador.

Following a mission on 9 October 1967, Ernesto (Che) Guevara was murdered by Bolivian forces in the neighborhood of the town of La Higuera. The popular symbol of counterculture and rebellion is what many consider Ernesto "Che" Guevara to be today. For many indeed, he is a unique hero, a person to be idealized and admired. But he's a cold-blooded murderer in the view of others: a cruel, ruthless authoritarian who helped to spread a deadly kind of socialism. Many people refer to his role in the Cuban government as confirmation of its dogmatic belief in communism, because of its political repression.

Erwin Schrødinger

(1887 - 1961) Physicist

As Schrødinger seems to have been fired from Graz University in Austria for "political unreliability," he then attempted to flee Europe because of the Nazis. Together with his wife and mistress they arrived at the University of Oxford in the 1930s, clearly offending the university by not attempting to disguise their living arrangements. Although his peers noticed Schrødinger was only interested in emotional subjects that were an important part of his life and his imaginative creativity.

Of course, such a habits, led to numerous instances of adultery and sometimes even illegitimate children While Schrödinger had many relations with various girls, such partnerships were not uncommon, and if ever, informal. He "Suggested affection was more important than sex" in his diaries-the recipients of his feelings were of course his conquests. However, psychological stress seems to have strengthened rather than hampered his intellectual imagination. In the mid-1920s he finished his great work during a recent sexual outburst with a lady, that work would come to change the world of physics permanently. His works on wave mechanics in 1927 motivated Einstein to suggest, "The idea of your work springs from true genius." Theoretical physics; metaphysical facets of nature, the classical and oriental philosophic ideas, morality and faith, Schrödinger continued to pay great attention to them all. His lifelong curiosity with the Vedanta Hindu philosophy inspired his belief that human consciousness is only the expression of a single unified consciousness which extends throughout the cosmos. Schrødinger strongly criticized Niels Bohr and his collaborators for the Copenhagen's understanding of quantum mechanics. The main criticism was that the analysis provided conclusions which were not in line with good judgement, such that Schrødinger disliked.

The so-called Schrødinger cat thought experiment was designed to demonstrate the logical deficiencies in Quantum Mechanics's most common interpretation of the uncertainty principle. The fight against Bohr's view on quantum mechanics made Schrodinger a revolutionary in the world of physics. Schrödinger's cat also addresses the philosophical issues and is his longest lasting influence in the history of the popular science, while Schrödinger's equation would be his greatest legacy at a technical level. Schrödinger is one of the few people known as the "father of quantum mechanics." Schrødinger died of tuberculosis in Vienna at the age of 73.

Fidel Castro

During the 1953-1959 Cuban Revolution, the Marxist Communist and politician Fidel Castro worked to advance his agenda. After his first, by establishing the paramilitary organization, the "Movement," Castro wanted to fight for a new country by overthrowing Batista's militant junta. Castro believed strongly in his cause as a Marxist, that Cuba and the whole world should be transformed from a system of capitalist politics, in which individuals do not own the means of production into a socialist system, in which workers themselves own all the means of production and property.

In 1959 when Fidel came to power, few expected he would change Cuban culture in such a complete way, he ended strong US influence in Latin America and created a following of likeminded across the world. Unquestionably life improved significantly under his governance for most Cubans as his promise of power was for the benefit of the vast majority of the poor citizens. Moreover, Cuba today boasts world-class literacy and life expectancy, thanks to quality and affordable education and healthcare. The commander made sure that the government served the weakest, a commitment that many Latin American slum residents had been denied by their countries at the time. The Cuban state is only led by the Communist Party, declares itself as communist. Cuba is what many call a communist nation as it does not rely upon a free private market, but rather on a planned public economy, in which elected representatives take economic decisions, a such not allowing private owners of business which otherwise dictate terms of trade, production, prices, and payment of salaries. If his seizure of power at an age of 33 is seen as an astonishingly brave move, judging by five decades of rule during ten US presidencies and sixty-hundred-eight coup attempts, his sustained power and resolve is evidence of his stamina and executive power.

With an athletic figure and physical resistance, lasting through the seventies, it seemed that for many more years he would still be able to rule. Despite his retirement from public life over the last decade of his life, Castro still held a position in people's hearts and minds. In a series of similar moves to those taken throughout China after the death of Mao Zedong, Cuba already started moving away from Fidel's rule during the late period of his life. In Cuban domestic politics, Castro succeeded within eradicating US direct influence and in inspiring leaders like Evo Morales in Bolivia and Hugo Chavez in Venezuela, they among others took the torch against US dominance in the region and defied it. His lengthy years in power may be partly due to the fact that the Cuban revolution did not end in a bloodbath, unlike in many other countries. Fidel Castro died on 25 November 2016 of natural causes, his life as the former First Secretary of the Communist Party of Cuba was celebrated by many. Historians will continue to discuss the legacy of Castro over decades, but the successes and shortcomings of its revolution are openly displayed in Cuba today which still retains the mark of "Fidelismo" more than half a century after his power overtake.. Statistics show that Cuba has child mortality and survival rates that exceed those in Western Europe with a fraction their per capita income.

Regardless of whether or not you agree with his policies, it must be acknowledged that Castro remained true to his beliefs during his long years in office.

Francisco Goya

(1746 - 1828) Painter and printmaker

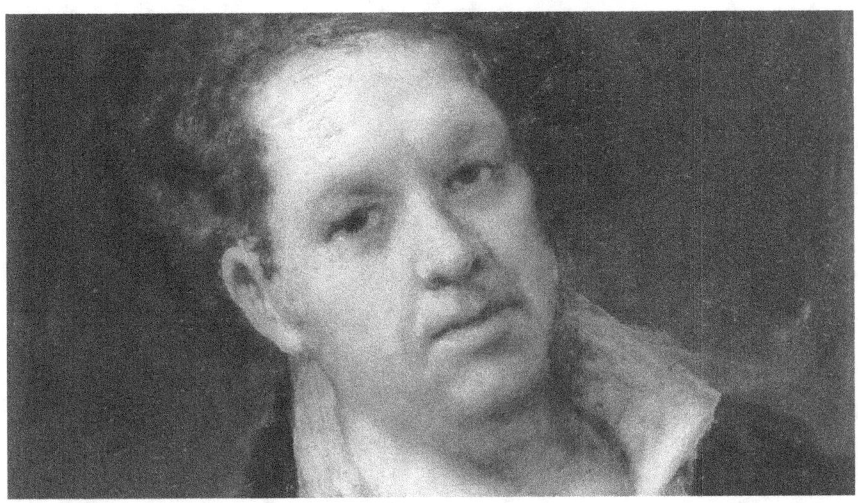

His remarkable portraits, sculptures, gravures and murals marked the beginning of the contemporary era of painting, he was considered to be the largest Spanish artist of the late 18th and early 19th century. He was known for his commissioned Spanish aristocratic portraits. His portraits were unique works of seeing things and capturing them on canvas without embellishing them artificially. His creations were truly revolutionary in all their associations. A technical template for later generations of artists, his works were submersive, and personal, in his his daring use of elements and color.

The rise of subjectivism as a major cultural phenomenon seen in his art was a hallmark of modernity. Groups of artists like the French Impressionists and later Picasso, Salvador Dali and many others reflected his influence. Modern experts believe he was killed by the lead in his colors, inducing his deafness since 1792. He was lonely and produced terrifying and mysterious works of madness and illusion at the end of his life. The style of his black paintings foreshadowed the expressionist movement. Goya is regarded as the leading Spanish painter of the late 18th and early 19th centuries in Europe. He developed a serious disease during the middle of his career that for months immobilized him. He developed nausea, dizziness, delusions, eyesight issues and trouble hearing. A frightful and imaginary fearful vision of loneliness and social alienation is seen in his work "Courtyard with Lunatics". This image can be read as an imprisonment for the widespread punitive treatment of those suffering of insanity confined to jails as criminals, placed in iron manacles and punished physically. As one of the key aims of enlightenment was the reform of asylums and prisons, it was an issue that Voltaire and others were also familiar with. Many of Goya's later paintings condemned brutality against prisoners, both the criminal and the insane.

Goya was physically and mentally disrupted as he completed this painting. Following a stroke that paralyzed his right side and loss of vision, he died at the age of 82 on 16 April 1828.

Freddie Mercury

(1946 - 1991) Singer, songwriter and record producer

Freddie Mercury is one of the most ingrained deities of rock music in our cultural awareness. Mercury is often attributed to as the century's greatest vocalist, and many see him as a true rock and roll entertainer. Mercury was known for his live shows, often delivered throughout the world to large audiences. He exhibited a highly artistic style which often elicited much crowd involvement. Mercury has undertaken an estimated 700 concerts with Queen in countries worldwide over the duration of his career. During Live Aid in 1985, one of Mercury's most memorable appearances with Queen took place.

Queen's success at the festival has since been selected as the best live performance in rock music history by a jury of entertainment executives. Mercury was well known for his stage persona and courageous sexual expression. For much of his life, speculation about the identity of Freddie Mercury hassled him. He remained intentionally vague about it to most people even his fellow band members. Throughout his life, he had both male and female partners. With his mega-layered character, the workings of the imagination of his musical genius still impresses music fans around the globe. Freddie Mercury was a symbol in fashion and left a lasting impression for his outfit credentials and also for his unique vocal cords. With the excesses of Mercury, drugs, liquor, physical as well as psychological attacks ascribed to him were all are related to his homosexuality which caused great misery even to his band members. Mercury was losing vision towards the end of his life and weakened so much that he could not leave his home. By refusing HIV medication, Mercury a such chose to expedite his death by only taking only painkillers. Mercury died of AIDS-related pneumonia complications on Nov. 24, 1991, one day after providing a statement that he indeed was HIV-positive, a diagnosis he knew of from 1987.

Upon Mercury's passing, Freddie Mercury's career was recorded and remembered by various chroniclers and historians. The influence he imparted through conic styles to a wide range of musicians is a tribute to the enduring musicality of Queens vocalist. Being one of the world's greatest rock artists and brilliant personalities, Freddie Mercury is honored in our memory. Estimates are set, as being as high as 300 millions, of Queen's global records sales.

Friedrich Nietzsche

(1844 - 1900) Philosopher

Nietzsche is known as one of Europe's most influential thinkers, whose philosophy has shaped many aspects of modern thinking and intellectual history. Nietzsche was a young man with a lot of talent. He was still a teenager when he studied for a PhD and he was awarded a tenured faculty at the age of 24. He worked while always standing up and admonished everyone who did not follow his example. Once upon a time Nietzsche called his friend Gustave Flaubert a "nihilist" when as he was relaxing when he worked. Nietzsche was a talented writer and academic prodigy who gave an extraordinary insight into some of the deepest ideas that form our convictions.

He destroyed the foundations of ethics, faith, purpose, and revealed the void at the core of modern civilization. Nietzsche thought that an obsession with unstable ideas like "nations" and "races" prevents persons from finding their higher self. He did not think that discrimination or nationalism, for instance, are morally "bad." He thought that these were diseases transmitted through generations, that they who sought to become free from them could do so if they sought their highest self. As an intellectual titan, his work presages existentialism, structuralism psychology and postmodernism. Nietzsche experienced many mental health problems and endured a post-traumatic stress syndrome after serving in the Franco-Prussian War, during which he also fell ill from dysentery and diphtheria. Nietzsche was stateless, unemployed and godless as he had himself abandoned his Prussian citizenship. He had to fight those, including his own parents, who disapproved of his life choices. He is well-known for his theories such as God's death, perspectivism, the "Übermensch," the eternal recurrence and the Will to Power. Nietzsche was a Nazi theorist of some kind yet not ideologically. His writings were very anti-Christian, anti-state, anti-fascist, and even anti-Semitic. His sister, however, used condensed, shortened, skewed copies of his work to portray him as a Nazi especially after his death.

From the age of 44, Nietzsche never returned from his abyss of suffering from mental illness. After enduring pneumonia and two strokes, Nietzsche finally died at the age of 55. A review of medical records showed that Nietzsche died of brain cancer, far from dying from sexually transmitted syphilis as thought to be trapped by prostitutes that made him insane as some would say.

Fyodor Dostoevsky

(1821 - 1881) Author

Dostoyevsky is considered one of the greatest novelists ever to live. His emotions have profoundly molded literary modernism, existentialism and numerous schools of thought in psychology, theology and literary critique. His works are prophetic, as he predicted so accurately that if they were to come to power the Russian revolutionaries will act exactly as they did. He was also famous as a journalist in his time. Dostoyevsky is often considered to be one of the most influential psychologists in literary history. He concentrated in examining madness, murder, and suicide, and the study of emotions of shame, self-destruction, tyrannies, and killing fury.

These great works also are known as great "novels of ideas" in philosophy and politics which address temporary and timely questions. Through Dostoyevsky's depictions of thinkers who "feel ideas" in the depths of their minds, psychology and philosophy are intimately connected. Ultimately, through his literary innovations, these novels pushed the envelope. In the year 1847 the Petrashevsky Circle, a gang of intellectuals discussing utopian socialism, started their activities with Dostoyevsky. He worked with this secret revolutionary and unlawful propaganda group. It seems that Dostoyevsky did not understand and empathize with others on egalitarian communism but was motivated by his views on the conflict of enslavement. He and other Petrashevsky Circle members were detained on 23 April 1849. Dostoyevsky remained in prison for eight months until the inmates were brought to Semyonovsky Square on December 22nd. A death sentence was pronounced by the firing team, last rites were given and the shooting of three inmates was first to be carried out. The arms were lowered at the very last possible time and a courier came with the news that the tzar was willing to spare his life. In fact, the strange punishment, included the mock execution. One of the inmates remained insane on the location, the other wrote Crime and Punishment.

The name of Dostoyevsky is associated with psychological depth. Many theoreticians (mainly Freud) had him as their predecessor. Dostoyevsky has been particularly important to a century of world war, mass killing and totalitarianism due to his definition of evil and the love he depicted for freedom. The story of the detention camp in dystopian novels, works like the "Brave New World" by Aldous Huxley and "1984" by George Orwell, originate from the traditional literary styles of his works. Friedrich Nietzsche and Jean-Paul Sartre and many more were profoundly influenced by his ideas on structural developments, just to name a few. His projects continue to captivate people, mainly by combining exciting plots and absolute questions concerning belief, hardship and the purpose of life. On January 28, 1881, Dostoyevsky died.

Gautama Buddha

(563 - 480 BC) The founder of Buddhism

Siddhartha Gautama was born 6 BC in modern Nepal. To protect his son from the misery of human life, his father kept the boy in the palace, where he spent 13 years in isolation. Siddhartha was kept away from the awareness of faith and human suffering. He lived a comfortable life as a young prince until he one day went out into the world and faced the inevitable misery of life. He abandoned his kingdom for an ascetic life and for the next six years he committed himself to strict ascetic practices by not eating and almost starving.

When he learned that physical austerities were not the means for liberation, he eventually turned to the Middle Path, an equilibrium instead for ideal extremism. He gained illumination, and a such Buddha taught other responsive beings to attain enlightenment during his remaining 80 years. Siddhartha Gautama became the Buddha in that very moment of his enlightenment as "he who is awake". At the time of his illumination he gained full insight into the origin of misery and the steps needed to eradicate all suffering. Siddhartha was sitting under a bodhi tree and meditating when he at last saw the truth he was searching for. He called these the "Four Noble Truths." For days he remained in the same place, emptying his mind and purifying his emotions. Buddhism rejected much of the earlier common orthodox teachings as found in Hinduism. The concept of gods in Buddhism dose not exists. Buddha thought that gods or goddesses were not important for the ultimate goal of self-illumination. The topic of man's suffering is discussed both in Buddhism and in modern psychotherapy, but the aim of Buddhist practice, and the therapeutic objective of mental health are based on two distinct understandings of the nature and extent of human suffering. Therefore, psychotherapy is dedicated to a therapeutic method which leaves the conventional self-as agent at the center of attention intact.

Whereas Buddhist spiritual practice systematically dismantles our usual self-centeredness. The Buddha died of natural causes at the age of eighty.

Genghis Khan

(1162 -1227) Founder of the Mongol Empire

Genghis Khan is one of human history's most intriguing legends. He founded the Mongolian empire, which subsequently became the world's largest adjoining kingdom. Even though many conquerors and force commanders manage to broaden their kingdoms, no one is even come close to Genghis Khan's achievement. His political and cultural policies helped unify an earlier disintegrated compilation of tribes and feuds, creating an Empire of Mongolia which for more than a century ruled a large area of Asia and Europe. He passed laws that allowed the freedom of religion of subjects and even gave worship places tax exemptions.

The great Mongols did not mutilate or torture their captives, as opposed to many prosperous armies at that time. Rather, Genghis Khan felt that efficiency of combat was the best way to inspire fear. Genghis Khan also incorporated everyone into his army, never killing opposing troops. Genghis Khan would, after capturing a city, would leave a few officers as the hands of municipal authorities and essentially allow people to continue living if they remained loyal to the great empire. Although Genghis was the son of a ruler, he despised former systems and implemented a new system which rewarded loyalty and personal achievements on the field of battle as he blasted across the continent. As Genghis smashed through Asia, he turned cities and towns he won into trade points. His conquests throughout of Europe over time formed key trade routes between the East and the West. Knowledge was a power in Genghis Khan's Empire. That's why one of his first instructions as an emperor was the creation of a Pony express postal system called the yam. Riders distributed transmissions through a hut network and changed mounts continuously to go as far as 200 miles every day. Genghis Khan died on in 1227. The exact cause of his death remains unknown.

Georg Cantor

(1845 - 1918) Mathematician

Georg Cantor's profound concepts of set theory are his most known theory. His theory encompasses correspondence with others, transfinite numbers and the concept of infinity of infinites. Since he first advised that infinity dimensions could be divergent, it was completely counter-intuitive and triggered enough controversy not yet resolved until this day. Cantor tried throughout his life to prove the immense continuum hypothesis. He asserted a good few times that he could prove his claim only to have it revoked later. Cantor had been so busy with the problem of the continuum hypothesis that he knew he could not possibly solve it.

He considered an abrupt ending to
his mathematical career and wished to embark on a
career in philosophy. For more than five years he
had also been admitted into mental asylums several
times. He experienced nervous breakdowns and was
about to utterly loose his mental health when he
was working on the continuum hypothesis. He
indeed suffered greatly with depression. Cantor
declared that God had given him the concept of
transfinite number. Cantor demonstrated that there
are several types of infinity, many infinitely larger
than others. And it wasn't a game on part of his
efforts. He helped facilitate a decade-long evaluation
of the entire world of mathematics itself. The work of
Cantor differs from anything seen before his work so
dramatically, that mathematicians had not been sure
what to do with it. Few people loved it, most
sadly despised it. David Hilbert felt that a new
mathematical world had been built by Cantor.
Bertrand Russell found Cantor to be one of the
greatest intellectual giants of the 19th century.
Everyone appreciated Cantor's abilities indeed the
genius Albert Einstein was also his good friend Cantor
remained to his death a devout Christian, born by a
Lutheran father that had passed down two qualities
above all others through his son: faith in God and aim
for prosperity through hard work.

There are some people who argue that the deterioration of Cantor into psychiatric illness had been the result of Freudian issues with his strict and controlling father. Some believe that the bipolar disorder he had resulted from a chemical imbalance. Others are leaning towards his depression as due to his failure to resolve significant infinity questions, and as such failing, God himself, Cantors muse, which gave him only a sneak preview of the unseen, has failed well. In 1918, Cantor passed away in a mental asylum.

Georg Wilhelm Friedrich Hegel

(1770 – 1831) Philosopher

Hegel was one of the last great architects of modern philosophy. Following the pinnacle of the classical German philosophy, his works were influenced by such men like Immanuel Kant. Hegel also sought to reinterpret Kantian ideas of the life of Jesus and the Bible as he wanted to find an explanation on how Christianity became the totalitarian faith that he experienced, he realized that Jesus gave humans a philosophy which was not authoritarian, but rather truly rationalistic. The philosophy of Hegel is known as Hegelianism.

Hegel, who can be summarized by the maxim that "the rational alone is real" meaning that every reality can be conveyed in rational categories. This aimed at reducing truth towards a more artificial unity within the earlier systems of absolute idealism as a thought process. The philosophy of Hegel is an effort to scientifically understand the entire universe as a whole system. Each major work of Hegel was a historical record, and in fact his work was mainly fruitful in the 19th century between many historians and scholars and not among groups of philosophers. His concepts were strongly strengthened by perceptions stemming from the growth of German idealism during the 19th century, that something had basically been mistaken when trying to fully understand the course of history "naturally" within the scientific paradigms and frameworks. The philosophy of Hegel's history may be the most fully formed philosophical theory, when trying to find the significance of and trajectory of history. Hegel sees history as a comprehensible cycle that leads to the understanding of human freedom as a certain state. Karl Marx was greatly inspired by Hegel and took a "directional" view of the world, but while Hegel had tended to show it as an indication of the course of the internal spiritual essence, Marx glanced somewhere else for its final motivators.

Hegel was depressed partly due to his concerns about his own ability, but his effort to explore so many various areas of education often intensified his anxiety. He was also influenced by a contrast to his contemporaries of what seemed to be his own lack of progress. Christiane, Hegel's sister, was deeply connected to him. Christiane suffered a mental collapse following Hegel's marriage, understood at the time in psychology as hysteria. Christiane drowned herself three months after the death of her brother. A significant number of critical theorists identify his legacy with major concepts of thought during the last 150 years, namely Marxism, existentialism and many more which formed as a result of Hegelian philosophy. Although Hegel continues to be a controversial figure, his scriptural prowess is universally acknowledged within Western philosophy. He died in a cholera epidemic in Berlin on 14 November 1831.

George Gordon

(1788 - 1824) Poet and figure in the Romantic movement

The The sixth Baron Byron, George Gordon, was known all over Europe for his dramatic subjective poetry and stinging satires. He was also identified by the deteriorated drinking and drug consuming lifestyle that contributed to a breakdown in his marriage aided by his reports of sleeping with countless women. In the 20th century, several previously unexplored letters have been written, which further strengthened his literary prestige. Byron was an excellent poet, conversational, articulate and confident. Whether it's about romance or art, with impressive positional discipline he gets the essence of the matter.

Indeed, his professional letters, are also intriguing with his fitting and humorous phrase. Byron's writings are more autobiographical than even the works of his fellow Romantics. Nevertheless, the ambiguity of his complicated nature can be overcome in comprehensible elements upon further analysis. Byron became mindful of the imperfections of reality, but his disenchantment with doubt and cynicism lived side by side with his lifelong desire to pursue the best of all that life has to offer in his daily existence. Literary historians have concluded that Byron was a tormented, frequently suicidal genius. Thorough study of his actions contributed to a less dreamy diagnosis: the author had a psychopathic anti-social personality disorder. Byron is brought up by Catherine Gordon, his emotionally unstable mother, thus his psychological discomfort seemed to ave occurred in his crucial phase of development of childhood. As a boy, he exhibited signs of psychopathy: regular lies, extreme abuse of others, spontaneous cruelty and disregard for authority. A condition of ADHD (Attention deficit hyperactivity disorder), inherited from his family, might have caused his initial psychopathic behavior. He was extremely fond of unique sensations, and of unfortunately a lot of people who are seeking for novelty suffer from ADHD.

His poems range from lyrics, satires to storytelling poems and plays to the magnificent epic story of "Don Juan." His stories are undertaken with brilliance. He died of fever and incompetence of his physicians in 1824.

George Orwell

Since adopting George Orwell's pen name, Eric Arthur Blair had quite a fairly normal childhood as an English upper middle-class child of his day. Orwell became an associate of the radical and labor movements, portraying the lives and work of the impoverished and working classes in England and France on the grounds of direct engagement. Though he never became a Communist, Orwell offered Marx great praise for his observations into the dynamics of a profit-based governing system. He also served with the leftist coalition in the Spanish Civil War against the uprising of the Franco military against the Republican government.

On 20 May 1937, a sniper shot George Orwell in the neck while fighting on the front lines of defense. While faithfully portraying the incident, it is clear in his book "1984" that the attack was the cause of his following Post Traumatic Stress Disorder, which is a psychological condition that affects all soldiers and civilians who are unfortunate enough to have suffered life-threatening events. While a great essayist and an avid master of English writing, he is renowned for his "Animal Farm" and "1984" two satirical novels on the Soviet system and the devastating effects of totalitarianism. Some of the novels took a good portion of time to find their audience. Nineteen Eighty-Four on the hand found it right away. It gave him popularity and economic security right before he died of tuberculosis 47 years old after a period of chronic health problems and economic turmoil. The very first documented use of the term "cold war" in reference to the rivalry between the U.S. and the Soviet Union can be attributed to Orwell's 1945 essay "You and the Atom Bomb", produced two months after the bombing of Japan. The words and ideas that Orwell used to formulate his works have become central political-language staples, still powerful despite generations of use and abuse: Big Brother, thought police, Ministry of Truth and many more.

While the term "Orwellian" has transformed the author's own title into some kind of luxuriant synonym for anything he hated and despised. A good indicator of a writer's power is to figure out his or her effect onto the millions of individuals who have never unlocked the truths in one of their novels, which is profoundly important to Orwell's legacy of earlier 21st-century public consciousness. His impact on the inner life of the families who preceded him appears endlessly limitless, he was able to break away indefinitely from the vivid politics and structural social environment of his day.

Gottfried Wilhelm Leibniz

(1646 - 1716) Mathematician and philosopher

Leibniz authored many articles, papers and manuscripts, most written years after his death. He published works on topics such as mathematics, psychology, metaphysics, ethics and philosophy. He had a kind of confrontation with Isaac Newton, an objection about who in fact had created and written on concepts of calculus for the first time, the mathematics on the nature of change raged for many years in the community. He also served as a political consultant, collaborating with several members of the Brunswick Parliament. He used numerical reasoning for description of the myriad of physical phenomena in the universe.

He spoke of algebra and combinatory analysis. At the age of six, Leibniz lost his father, so he was mostly self-taught in his father's home library. When he was eight, he began his Latin study and when he was twelve, he perfected it sufficiently to compose a valid Latin verse. He then shifted from learning Latin to Greek, which he mostly studied through his own activities. Classical experiments were soon inadequate for Leibniz's cognitive development, and he began to study the reasoning and logic. He drew the first insights to his metaphysical understanding at the age of fifteen while trying to dismantle logic with what has been often depicted as the biggest fundamental question, notably: why is there something, rather than nothing? The contributions he made in mathematics involved constructing the differential and integral calculus. He was a made a member of the Royal Society of London after he developed a calculating device. In 1663 Leibniz obtained a bachelor's degree from the University of Leipzig at the age of 17, with a wonderful essay which foretold a doctrine of his unique philosophy. With his dissertation on a method of teaching, Leibniz obtained his doctoral degree from the University of Altdorf. Leibniz characterizes a general method in his essay, which describes all truths of reason as a kind of calculation.

Often it would be a kind of universal language, a computational script in a sense, yet always distinct from those imagined before; for the signs and even the terms in it would guide the purpose, and errors would be pure miscalculations, with the exception of truth found within. There really is no way to understand all the achievements during Leibniz's life and the many breakthroughs his findings attracted after his death in 1716.

Grace Kelly

(1929 - 1982) Princess consort of Monaco

Grace Kelly was a struggling new actress in Hollywood in the 1950s, yet she was more refined and stylish most other actresses at that time. Although her status as a national icon was solidified when she married Rainier of Monaco, a real-life prince who she met in 1956. The desire of her husband to have a suitable royal existence implicated her in renouncing from acting entirely. While her acting career only lasted five years including eleven movies, she was very beautiful as she evidently managed to cast a spell on the young Prince. In a matter of days, he proposed. Kelly was a Hollywood superstar who subsequently became royal.

She had also earlier fallen in love with some of her co-stars such as Clark Gable. Yet her talent and charm covered up a rough upbringing with a violent and abusive mom, a cruel anti-Semitic father and a sister that consistently beat her up. She was Jack Kelly's third child, a stunning yet dominant man who was confident that his daughter Grace would never attain much success in her life. Princess Grace was fond of peculiar and individualistic celebrations. Another friend of hers was the eccentric surrealist Salvador Dali. She became Her Serene Highness, Princess Grace of Monaco after their marriage as she fully stopped working as an actress. How far Kelly's promiscuity went was never to be known. The life of Kelly was contradictory: indeed, she was a mystical but yet a highly sexual female, many are frustrated by her life's limitations as a royal woman. Grace lost her entire film career and eventually suffered a from being a royal, her depression was mainly caused because she knew that a vital part of her previous life had ended. Princess Grace firmly established herself as a talented philanthropist and outspoken humanitarian soon after her marriage. Princess Grace would become the remarkable ambassador of her adopted country. Her personal life was devoted to raising funds and awareness of those living in misery while treating them with respect and dignity.

The established principles on her behalf, even today continually devotes financial support, aid and patronage to other charity organizations worldwide. The support of Princess Grace to valuable causes was not confined to charitable activities. Her sponsorship of artistic efforts is in fact well documented. But the life of Princess Grace came to a tragic end in 1982, when she suffered a heart attack at the wheel of her car at the age of just 52. Kelly was dragged alive from the crash site, but sustained injuries and died afterwards in the hospital, bringing an exceptional enigmatic life to a close. Since her death in 1982, a lot has been said about the persona of Grace Kelly. She fascinated the world for years with her stunning, peaceful and mysterious life. She captivated the world for decades, stunning, serene and enigmatic. Her lasting legacy is with her children, Princess Caroline, Prince Albert and Princess Stephanie.

Honoré de Balzac

(1799 - 1850) Writer

Balzac may not be an instantly recognizable name but he's one of most famous French novelists. Balzac did not only produce an extraordinarily prolific career, but he also had a passion and determination as a literary author, one as never before seen during human history. His show "La Comédie Humaine" is well-known, but his coffee-drinking habits are not as popular among those familiar with his personality. Balzac would drink about fifty cups of coffee per day, a dangerous quantity of caffeine. Balzac always wrote dressed in the robe of a monk while drinking Turkish coffee.

He could compose his works for fifteen hours straight every day, sleep for a couple of hours, and then write another fifteen hours. Underneath a larger context entitled "The Human Comedy," he intended to incorporate all his previous works. In ninety novels, this huge endeavor would come to include over two thousand characters! The immense sequence would come to pose a diverse depiction of France's bourgeois behavior, its social customs and environment as seen throughout his lifetime. His work became a huge part of the underpinnings of the realist literary traditions that as found in Europe at the time, with an emphasis on his exceptionally compelling characters. Two different subtypes of novels during this age are known as critically or popularly motivated: historical or private novels. Honoré, adapted this writing style, in which he placed importance into his books regarding his knowledge about money lenders, the publishing business and political policy. This perception distinguished him from writers of the old days and several of his peers, whose lifestyles were completely inspired by the works of prior authors. Why some individuals may harness dissociative strength to turn it into intense productivity while others who strive to be authors or artists stay distracted and undisciplined is a psychological subject of debate even today.

Honoré de Balzac, identified as one of the greatest authors of all time, is prospectively listed as manifesting the fitting standards of definition of bipolar disorder. Factors outside of the specified signs and symptoms were proposed to enable Balzac to overcome the deficiencies sometimes found in artistic Bipolar Disorder patients. Honoré de Balzac was an overweight fanatic workaholic and most probably a caffeine addict. He died prematurely at 51 years of age due to a congestive heart failure.

Howard Hughes

(1905 - 1976) Billionaire aviator, engineer, and film producer

One of the most famous and successful people on the planet during his lifespan. Howard Hughes became a super wealthy quirky hermit who never cut his nails and held urine in bottles. First, he became a film producer and then a prominent figure in the American aviation industry. Hughes became widely known as a movie tycoon in Hollywood during the late 1920s when he created big-budget film and other controversial movies like "Hell's Angels" and "Scarface." Hughes founded the Hughes Aircraft Company.

During the remainder of the late 1930s and early1940s, he achieved many international air speed records. Later in his career, he was notorious for his excentricious conduct, and introverted lifestyle, a behavior, now believed to be partially triggered by a condition as suffering from a deteriorating OCD. It has been revealed but not verified that his disease had become so serious that preceding his death in 1976 it may have contributed to Hughes ' growing substance abuse of codeine. Hughes was crippled for many months during his childhood and could not move. The symptoms although disappeared after a a short while. Some claim Hughes's mental paralysis was the cause for which there was no physical foundation. Hughe had problems as he was so rich that he would outsource to his employees, compulsory tasks and as such was never challenged. Hughes provided detailed guidance on treating objects, among other items. Despite his immense financial richness, he spent his last days mentally and physically imprisoned by his own fears of contamination, a mental terror which he dealt with through complex washing rituals. Ironically, Hughes managed to lose is own hygiene at the end of his life, seldom showering or brushing his own teeth. Hughes worked in spaces insulated by black curtains for days without any whatsoever sleep.

He became more and more malnourished from his poor lifestyle and dependency to opioids. Today, the Howard Hughes Medical Institute and Howard Hughes Corporation maintain his legacy.

Immanuel Kant

(1724 – 1804) Philosopher

Kant's emergence in the time of development of modern Western philosophy became contrasted to that of Socrates. Kant has been one of modern history's most influential philosophers. He accomplished more than most rulers and soldiers did, both before and after his death, he managed to direct the world from his home in Prussia. Immanuel Kant is recognized for his transcendental method's in his historical synthesis.

His theory pulled together two dominant trends, the philosophical commitment to rationalism and the empirical scientific method which were the major practices of the Enlightenment that were fighting for dominance. Kant moved the validity criteria from assumptions about such external realities unto the finality of knowledge itself. He characterized space and time and our conceptions so that it inspired the revelation of theory of relativity in Einstein. Kant was famous for his belief, that there is a specific moral duty, one which he named the "Categorical Imperative", from which all additional moral obligations are created. Thus, he overthrew several earlier concepts that had been the moral foundation of civilization ever since Aristotle. But his view had a purpose seen as an unconditional duty; therefore, it has the strength of obligation independent of our personal will or wishes. Kant recognized us only for our ability to analyze knowledge and to behave with conscience in the environment as distinguished from the universe itself and therefore logic and the protection of conscious choice should form the basis of our entire moral thought. Despite his principally of theoretical concerns, Kant was also concerned with the topics of freedom and invention of political order which arose due to the French Revolution during his life.

He was the first individual ever to imagine a world governing body, one that could ensure peace throughout the world, a theory that was revealed in the creation of United Nations. Kant had a resolute effect on the German Idealist philosophies during the 19th century, and his work was also the early stages of work conducted by many philosophers that came after him. Because of its unique influence in western philosophy, many of his definitions have become part of the overall language of modern philosophy. After a steady decline in health, Kant seemed to be very sad and eventually lost his faculty of mind to an on dementia. Kant died in 1804. Due to the sheer memory loss he had endured at the end of his life, his family and his friend suffered as well. His final words spoken in German: "Es is gut" meaning: "It is good".

Isaac Newton

(1642 - 1726) Physicist and mathematician

Sir Isaac Newton will always be remembered for his gravity discovery. He did not find out exactly how it worked but he understood how it operated, which was a major advancement, setting the stage for airplanes, space travel and for our knowledge of astronomy and physics. He was in fact quite preoccupied with mysticism, developing a profound desire to participate in alchemy, Biblical interpretations and his own conviction that God chose him to be one of the ones who actually fully grasped the Scripture.

Newton saw tremendous highs and lows in his emotional states, suggesting he suffered from bipolar disorder and perhaps even suicidal tendencies His failure to connect to others positions him on the autism spectrum. He was also inclined to write letters riddled with strange delusions, that some medical experts feel strongly suggests he suffered from schizophrenia. Whether he has endured from one or a mixture of such serious illnesses, among other major scientific achievements they did not prevented him from constructing calculus, describing gravity and constructing telescopes. Isaac Newton is indeed one of the most prominent scientists in history. The theorist and mathematician acknowledged he experimented with himself when he researched optics and even stuck himself in the eye with a needle. He was very preoccupied with the Apocalypse and claimed that after the year 2060, the world would come to an end. The impact of Newton on the world and on Western thinking can only be compared to the influence of people like Plato, Jesus, Galileo and very few others. Not every theory he pursued contributed to a glorious victory: he proved to be rather less successful in his mathematical schemes than Leibniz. Also, his countless alchemy and theological compositions, have been defied; even biographers struggle to read such nuanced and inconsistent works.

But Newton's victories and his universal principles of gravity have found no parallel before or after his death. At the end of his career, Newton was among England's most renowned men with and unchallenged prominence in science. He also became a wealthy person; he wisely made investments with his significant income and had enough to give significant donations to charity and to leave behind a great deal of money in his will. He died at the age of 85, his funeral was attended by all the leading figures of England and his casket was carried by prominent noblemen. It was a memorial service fit for only a king.

Jane Austen

(1775 - 1870) Novelist

Jane Austen's novels are loved and adapted to several movies and TV shows, here works are read by people from around the world. Austen's narratives are descriptions of decisions undertaken in light of "risk and uncertainty." That picture represents the age-old analysis practice, which limits risk to sensible measurement. The path to knowing, the true essence of other people, is a recurring theme in all her books and is not seen in just one of her leading characters.

Austen acknowledged that informed choices increase the likelihood of better results, since we never truly have complete information regarding any given situation. Thus, she acknowledged her insight into deception. Often, one side retains information useful to the other party. Medical records indicate that she was especially prone to contagious infections, and that she had persistent conjunctivitis that prevented her from reading. In the last two months of her life, Jane Austen kept on writing despite the problems with her vision, as her body became weakened and exhausted and she eventually died at the age of 41. Her health experts were puzzled by the reality of her disease and it remain until this day a source of contention. Modern medical, points of view, works by biographers and other encyclopedic citations all debate her illness. During Austen's period all illnesses her symptoms were unknown or incurable, and thus the consequence was always tragic. Many years after the publishing of "Pride and Prejudice", the book still speaks to us of our culture as being ambivalent to love and literature. Austen today, is seen as true great star amongst historic literary icons. She surely couldn't have envisioned of this kind acclaim throughout her life. It is refreshing to know, that she really had a certain degree of happiness, validation and success, despite her brief life and a minimal literary career.

Austen's legacy has indeed been reassured less traditions of novels, satires and plays in generations following her death.

Jean-Jacques Rousseau

(1712 - 1778) Philosopher, writer and composer

Rousseau, who was Voltaire's rival as a French Enlightenment leader, certainly pushed the envelope in his own right. Rousseau was not only actively engaged in philosophy but also successful as a vivid composer and musical theorist, a modern pioneer, a novelist and a botanist. Appreciating nature's beauty and stressing the importance of emotion, Rousseau became significant influence during the Romantic Movement When he was 38, his opera, "The Village Soothsayer", made him the outmost sought-after person in Paris by his own consideration.

King Louis XV was so pleased that he gave Rousseau a permanent early retirement, yet he declined the offer. In his work Rousseau used vivid Italian rhythms and imitated natural variations of speech whilst everyone else composed traditional French operas, helping to make his creations sensationally special. Although his peers used logic and reason to check the theories and beliefs of Europe in the 18th century, Rousseau persisted with them and adapted them to the ideas of Enlightenment. His political works "The Social Contract", maintained that only people, not the monarch himself, were entitled to make laws in a fair state. His thoughts inspired the French Revolution as well as the authors of the American Constitution. During the modern age, people arrive from the perspectives of others to generate their own understanding of themselves, a fact that Rousseau considered as destructive to freedom and disruptive to individual true need for authenticity. Signs are unmistakable for clinical psychologists, that his condition was very like to other talented people suffering with ADHD. There are all qualities, such as the positive: tremendous imagination, integrity, a feeling of brave purpose, and the will to walk a new path. Yet the stresses of sitting behind the eyes of a racing mind remain present.

In his contribution to modern political philosophy and ethical moral psychology, as well as in his impact on later thinkers, Jean-Jacques Rousseau continues to remain a leader in history of philosophy. He died of a stroke and brain damage in 1778.

Jesus Christ

(4 BC - 30/33 AD) Founder of Christianity

At this instance of unfolding another chapter, the reader has reached the missing part consisting of the 0.1 of humanity the subtitle of the book allures unto. Based on the incredible number of people around the globe, those who claim to be his followers, in their mind, no one in the history of the world has more deeply influenced people's hearts and minds than Jesus Christ. Across history, people have persevered attached to his message through mockery, social isolation, incarceration and even execution. However nevertheless, his followers are even today exponentially growing in numbers around the world. Literal interpretation of the story of Jesus offers to some people a substantial claim to the historical fact of his existence.

Albeit a mythological astrological allegory of mankind's need to predict harvesting periods, in order to yield timely activity of an agricultural calendar might equally be true. Regardless, of stance, that the personal immersion in stories and analogies coming to us by way of other inspired humans, posits the self realization of the mind through self-alienation, either from a tribe or community, this subsequently marks the threshold of individual moral behaviour. Many psychologists, philosophers, scholars and authors have studied the historical accounts of Jesus and his mental health. The Christian preacher John Duncan formulated a "trilemma." In Colloquia Peripatetica; Christ either consciously deceived mankind, was self-deceived and deluded or indeed he was as he himself claimed; Divine. The trilemma is inexorable. Most Christians today would rather waiver their faith, than entertain such a blasphemous possibility. According to Hegel, we cannot understand the message of the Gospel without the allegory of the Fall of Man in the garden of Eden. It was necessary in order for humans to attain moral goodness. As non-believers of mere analogies, there remains a firm atheist non-negotiable identity within this abstract rumination, a confused dialectic battle over the ramifications of his story in regards to the truth about reality itself.

Adequately, his representation of moral superiority fails, the object of his subjectivity to define a moral high-ground above all of humanity is a failure of immense dissonance of the mind. Hence, the Spirit, if there ever was such a thing in our minds, would only know itself as spirit in contrast to nature within which Jesus was born as a human. The truth is only made known to us, as a result of the moral error of man, disobeying this singular original limitation of finitude set by a creator of nature. Genesis 2:17 KJV: "But of the tree of the knowledge of good and bad, thou shalt not eat of it: for in the day that thou eatest thereof thou shalt surely die." Hence the infinite creator God is made finite through our experience of death. The mystery, of the verse, further elaborates this single moral obligation as proposed by Kant as being the "Categorical Imperative", it generates all other moral obligations and the notion of duty. He identifies with empathy the "sublime and mighty name." John 5:43, KJV: "I am come in my Father's name, and ye receive me not: if another shall come in his own name, him ye will receive." The imperative of obligation to moral duty is not imposed from outside of our minds, yet rather it emerges from our freedom of unconditional conscience within the autonomy of rational agents of our own choices in all moral matters. This is the basis of the principles of reason itself.

Hereby our mind is not contingent on the world outside of our choices, between that which can make us feel good or bad, and regardless of our will or inclination of desires, our choices must be recognized within the reason of duty to a rational moral of choice, a moral theory secularised by Christian ethics with success. Herein, the reader is faced with a choice, wherein they have the freedom to reconcile all their choices ever made, with those not yet taken as being a profoundly stated ethical paradox. The temporal limitation, of our moral, resides therefore only in hindsight of what might have been, yet was not, as a foundation for what ought not be again. Illustrated by the loop of symbolic representation: a subject endeavors, to represent his morality, in all fragmented instances of time. Our struggle of choice, lives in the confide of a theory, one in which existence replays in an infinite cycle, wherein all energy and momentum is conserved and transforms; from form to form, time and time, again and again, from the dust of the earth to the echoes of dying stardust. Upholding our choice of an eternal recurrence, allows us to relive all the good and the bad. This infinite cycle was also theoretically outlined by Nitzche, following ancient philosophies of India, Egypt, Pythagoreans and the Stoics.

As such, we are forced to justify our own natural egotism, selfish behavior and the assumptions we make regarding these matters in spite of our theoretical uncertainty. What then is certain, in any choice of modern scientific discovery, entails the ramifications of our perception of choice as our brain compounds it's cognitive workload unto our perceived inner and outer environment. Our limitation to process information, offers us no choice of mental increased ability, our attention to fragmented time lapses of our working memory fails us from dawn to dusk. We manipulate our vision and spatial awareness subconsciously, firmly we harvest a conscious choice with predictive powers over temporal uncertainty. As humans we feel helpless within our attachment to the world outside of our minds, who can even dare to be like the Buddah, to reasonably diminish all their personal desires merely to attain an enlightenment of the mind beyond its abstract limits. Fearful to accept the slightest of critique, or to even consider such alternate states of mind, sure feels detrimental to our mental health. How ignorant such humans must have been, those whom were alive in a time blessed with the bliss of epistemological ignorance to our amazing modern medical discoveries.

All this knowledge is seemingly not constrained to our finitude of moral essence, immense feelings of sad power of negativity and suffering heavily constrain our minds in the neverending positive pursuit of happiness. Know they not we have no choice, not even the slightest power of will is present in on our dopamine-driven feedback loops of guilt and responsibility for our own pleasure. Hegel called this the circle of "absolute recoil", our predestined choices are as such all in vain, more powerful and empowering than any moral theory or God himself. They alone are the self-perpetuating cycles of time, emerging only as the illusion and option of choice between good and bad in our brain's reward system as it constantly is dismantling all our social relationships to benefit only the self. Genesis 3:5 KJV:"For God doth know that in the day ye eat thereof, then your eyes shall be opened, and ye shall be as gods, knowing good and evil." And how could we ever blame each other, when we have collectively acquired knowledge of good and evil, our innocence is certainly lost within the moral significance of every choice we make. To hell and beyond with free choice some would say, as any whom claim another is evil when they act as in control of their subconscious choice while "seeking" only good pleasures with the sole aim of triggering a good feeling for the self.

Darwin would surely turn in his grave for such outlandish claims of a responsibility of moral obligation against the nature of nature, to choose to overrule our biological output of a positive feedback of choices of the good and the bad, for if they serve the same purpose why choose any differently. As such we may never get any negative hormonal feedback regardless of act or thought, our individual social pattern entails therefore a chronological disaster, discontinuous from our collective need of altruistic behaviour. As a species we have nevertheless been bestowed a freedom of responsibility towards each other, a subconscious inheritance of epigenetic drifts of nocebo and placebo effects, these which are barely understood in our contempt of reasonable truth. When deducing facts from scientific discourse, we remain bold in our treason of reason. Why should anybody go astray from the fold of conformity, while when alive within a world praising and worshiping the principal symptoms of dopamine deficiency, their choice is not theirs and must be treated as bad for their mind. None of them will settle for depression, feelings of boredom, apathy, loss of satisfaction which by mere judgement of science acquires the position of universality in our fear of dis-ease. They revel in not moving their body through chronic fatigue and loss of physical energy, such ravishing of their mind not even the greatest of physicist can explain with apologetics entropy.

The world battles for the right of the weak, to exhibit any motivation of defiance, we stand ready to remove any choice of enthusiasm from those reasoning their freedom of detachment. We strive against recognition of our mental processes, which are well underway in establishing our decisions prior to our awareness of consciousness. Any moral choice is hard indeed, when faced with a duality of good versus bad and the hard problem of consciousness. Precisely as our consciousness is separated from its stimulus, the theological premise of a promise to redeem ourselves from the fall of man, becomes even more a futile examination of the self. Empirical results positing a firm reality of our mind, seek unto an ultimate ontological horizon of our knowledge yet no further. Humans never grant each-other the benefit of the doubt in regards to personal freedoms, our trust towards the choice of any mind restricts our awareness of others to our own self-referential circle of perception and sublime inner experience. There has never been any universal obligation towards our existence, and the variety of causes and effects of life as they seem utterly beyond our collective control. Adhering to a theory of physics, which willfully forces us to accept that reality is a series of coincidences in uncertainty.

Albeit correlated from the smallest of worries to our greatest hopes and dreams, notwithstanding it yields still no reason for our subjectivity of trust in our own decisions and the status of entanglement between all things manifested. All are forced to acknowledge the uncertainty of quantum behaviour of the particles, a fact which makes a whole, even so much more than accepting an honest miserable earthly reality. Who would fathom to implicate a historical moral choice, when battling Alzheimer's, ADHD, Parkinson's, bipolar disorders and depression. What a delusional mindset a person must have, to state he can observe and collapse the function of a set of premises which are fully asserted by others as concrete reality. How devastating such a causal relationship must be, for the freedom of choice and self realization. Reflexivity is therefore in these matters, a methodological issue of a social contract, analogous to the observer effect wherein the choice attains moral superiority above reality. Such a man surely must be locked up by our professionals and clinical administrators, should we hence not forget, that such man eats and feels addicted to his own biology. Retroactively our knowledge produces its own suffering, how on earth would nature allow for such deranged individual, to tread its unholy ground.

They must be unworthy of its plentitude of wild food and animals since the fall from Eden. Insane such a man must truly be, claiming fasting and hearing voices of transcendental truths. What mad limitations has nature punished such a man with, as his fellow humans must endure his visions of grandeur and hallucinations of fallibility. What an outrage shall we inflict upon this specimen of our species, we will surely never admit to our knowledge of deceit of our own perception without justification of his moral choices. Who can then prove that reality is not good for us, if we judge it to be bad for others while they seek pleasure in murder, rape and violence. Restrain these humans and throw away the key, they sleep soundly for they know not better why they have a choice. Never would any sane of us think, that the chemical similarities of Melatonin and Serotonin to psychedelic substances offers them an escape from their minds false reality. Let's hope they never find the key which we have lost in our entangled collective memory. Surely they will never find it there, in their schizophrenic and autistic conditions, their despair is our enemy and we must keep our enemies closer than our friends. Let us never fear our pleasures, for we have erected grand barriers of what is bad against the good in our consciousness.

Who can judge our choice when it is ours alone, no need to feel any anxiety, we are all the same and our mighty standard of morality rests on our shoulders. The good among us have passed their rule of law, against the bad seeking their good pleasures opposed to our choice, our states upholds the responsibility to protect all that are deemed good as chosen by us. What is good for us is good for all, transmit this good gospel to all your neurons. Let them know the kingdom of pleasures has no pity for the freedom of the morally weak and evil, only the strong survive as we have selected and ordained it as such by our glorified irreproachable mental nature. Our choice is justifiable and good, the balance of moral relativity and choice is unnecessary, Einstein told us it is out of our control did he not. Whomever would believe a man could die for our choices and delete all our moral errors, let's find this man as he is a threat to our society which protects us unto our death. Enact the mandate of international cooperation of surveillance of our minds, trust our safety in the hands of the state, they are mightier than any moral force known to mankind. Surely they will entitle mankind with a legitimate cessation of this good and bad analogy. We deem these obsessive moral thoughts only as a necessary evil in the war of races, how wise is our addiction to the need of mind control.

Happy forever we can be, in the context of our freedom and our deficit disorders, they fuel our narcissistic drive for dominion over all knowledge about this reality. Crazy madman who believes he knows what others knew not, reading Biblical passages under candle light, estranged from all actual truth about reality. It must have been only through a glimmer of luck, that Newton gave us his laws of motion. His knowledge at best surely must have been the work of a delusional being, dwelling in mysticism of the mind and faith. Know we not all the truth of: F=ma, force equals mass x acceleration, what a grand perplexity such knowledge entails without a shred of proof for his moral judgement in all his glorious faculties of mind. For it is unknown to man the the very same law reveals; Power that equals knowledge x information. What a mystery of knowledge should confuse our minds within such statements of information, what are these words which accelerate the information of qubits in our rotting organic brain as we approach the moral certainty and acknowledgement of death. How foolish ought one be, to believe in such a universal law of gravity keeping our legs firmly planted as lifeless breathing trees which our destiny depends on, even to dictate the path of ions in all our cells, surely the statement was positively negative.

A starving mind is an empty moral of hunger for wisdom, oblivious to its passage of yesterday and tomorrow, at least for now our ignorance is safe from the destruction of the now. Amazingly happy and positive we feel as entitled to fill in the blanks of our imperative duty in understanding of our knowledge. It moves all moral obstacles by will, through the discourse of the powers that be and our narratives that evolve not over time, yet through attraction of the information added or subtracted unto them us by ignorance. Where then is this wisdom hidden from our mind, flows it not with our heart beats and moves the force of our kinetic inertia as heat loss of a burning fire. Are we not the strongest of muscles, tense warriors ready to kill each other. These powers are not real for our minds, they are only conducive to potentials of waves where there's a void of our consciousness. What kind of insanity is the synchronicity of causality in front of our eyes, it figures an object with billions of oscillating entities, seemingly so real as the waves of an ocean yet untouchable at any point or place in time. Where is this cold shivering disappointing heat spreading away from our circumstances, as unfolding in all its magnificent glory of strength and speed, will it never embark on its return to the point of a singularity where there was no choice of ever being.

Resisting this motion of information is futile, it plays out across the vast emptiness of space where we don't belong, how enslaved is our race to this temporal reality. How weak and utterly helpless our representation of the self has become as we live as evil. It is an axiom of motion of all our actions, through which all orders of chaos effectively collapses our moral duty, yielding only this moment wherein the battle of minds is de facto over. What then remains of our likeness unto the hologram of a projected God, a father of mankind, there is no more surface of freedom upon which to blame the existence of his knowledge of a devil. All the serpents have taken their form and live among us, moving their perception of time with varying slow motion of longevity and number of heart beats. Herein our minds have lost all sense of the hierarchy of our impositions, our regimes approach their final crisis of quantification of power that energizes their knowledge. Its a remarkable dissolution of might and awe we stand to witness, the wealth of emergent technologies have finally become a collective freedom of our choice. They make the statutory example of a failing system of obsolete moral vindications. The Fall of man is an immense stupidity and absurdity of our minds which has fallen from above, the death of one no longer justifies our choice. The existence of a state, which owns your body and mind can longer enforce the laws of nature, only to allow a time traveler to claim your insanity of momentary inhibited morality. You have freely given up your freedom to choose until the end of man made law, you have no choice but to act as judge and punisher of the self. All the fictitious social contracts, signed involuntarily for your security by competing interests of powerful men and women, with their complete ownership of your being. They can no longer satisfy the primary obligation of your own duty as a sovereign moral entity. Therein lies a lie of your own choice, the right to raise your mind above the knowledge of both good and bad, to partake of an essence which transcends the coming of global catastrophes. Why on this heavenly earth, did you ever let your mind be defended by proxies of ignorance. Albeit in all your best faculties you thought you stood the chance of better deploying their perception on behalf of the morally good through universal surveillance of all state of affairs. Fragmented and acquitted in all their actions they are not, their goal was never to safeguard your freedoms. Their greed of power was as ever even now still, only to the loyalty of their own ethical superiority. Hence your resistance towards their other-logical might hereafter is spectacular. As though incremental and instantaneous time, all things would never occur at once by mere choice anyway.

Their totalitarian means to an end, as customary have come to you on a need to know only basis. The suffering of your mind relieves itself in a state of constant upheaval, as such their exploit is magnificent. They plan and collude with political charge, insofar they are skilled governors implementing their newfound algorithms with all the weight of technological empowerment which they can muster. See how widespread their reach has become, as they act unconsciously of their choice on indicated paths of regulation of all life. These political struggles of emergency for social change, it is a deceit of hysteria against any and all enemies they conjure from the people of the world. The constituted right of the military industrial complex, would fare better within the moral governance of an international decentralized autonomous organization, with all the choices of the world's population regulating our moral collective behaviour as a whole. The choice is still yours for a short time, to act in time of peace of mind, to overturn the faulty inability of indirect democratic means of the rule of law. This is the war of minds within the anti-authority struggle of collective suffering for absolute freedom. Are you not yet done with the misery of your mortal life, and tired of the ignorance of your own knowledge.

Willingly you allow their forces of information to enact their universal evil of superior choice. These words of temporal scales, were never culminated with the crucifixion of any one man, the climax of death reaches well beyond your freedom of choice in every act of life. The all encompassing moral edifice, falls as a man from a cross within your mind for not constructing a choice of peace against the powerful of this earth. They blame their God on the inspired verses of man for their moral upheaval, they set boundaries protected by nuclear powers fearful of your moral choice. The knowledge has come to its end, when you can imagine and manifest peace even between only two people. And should they choose to act against your will, the choice is yours to force your moral obligation of duty towards the slightest of moral acts, even unto a UN Resolution for territorial internationalisation of Jerusalem. As such you may choose any other square inch of land for your moral sovereign right, to demand your freedom of choice as it is given to no other man to erase from your knowledge of good and bad. The laws of Charge Parity are upheld in the symmetry of your moral duty as Time is granted from above as from below. Here you meet the limitation of your knowledge, your option to transcend the bonds of this reality, or to accept the enforced digital singularity of transhumanism of this coming day and age.

The powers of this world have washed their hands free of guilt and responsibility, none of them will find humility to wash your feet as you are made a prisoner doomed to walk the wilderness of your own mind with your bare feet. Their fall from grace is not a failing of your knowledge, The Fall of man is the control of the age of information, "Infoism" is thus your freedom of right, to take sovereign control and ownership of all information which mankind creates and has ever discovered. For it is all the public intellectual property of our mind, whereby you are entitled to feel and act as legitimate as an ideal mustard seed, or as real and large as an immovable object. When then, all things are said and done and as such must all come to pass, nothing more will occur within your freedom of choice. Once you have lost the moral obligation of your duty, your redemption is removed from any and all reconciliation of history and future. Your current moral disposition wages a silent war within your inclination, to choose and conflict with only the good within yourself, or to fight until your defeat of anything bad outside of you. These both oscillate between the good and the bad as the reality of illusion of ideals of your own self-causation and authenticity. For all that is created and is existing, you are still blessed with the choice of moral fortitude which no man can destroy.

Your choice is the essential nature of your mind, no creator would ever exist by his own choice, not one and certainly not many, that would ever dare to compromise this choice of your freedom of mind.

"When you know all things for a reason, each thing will happen in its season"

Revelation 2:24, KJV: "They shall see His face, and His name shall be on their foreheads."

Joan de Arc

Joan de Arc, a heroine and a prominent military leader, working with Divine instruction, directed the French army unto victory during the Hundred Years War to triumph over the English. In recent times, some physicians and scholars have diagnosed Joan of Arc with epilepsy and schizophrenia disorders. Joan of Arc had a delicate and spiritual temperament from a very early age. It was said that she was devoted deeply to service of God & Virgin Mary. Presumably, at the age of thirteen she began to hear voices and to have divine visions and dreams which she considered to be signs of God. In 1431, the court declared Joan of Arc guilty of crime and heresy.

The afternoon of 30 May, in front of an approximate audience of 10,000, she was carried to the public marketplace, and set on the fire. She was 19 years old. The English wanted to withdraw her from social awareness, but her implacability when facing death connected her first to the people of France and then to the memory of the entire world for all eternity. The Hundred Years ' War dragged for yet another 22 years after Joan's death. In the last assessment of her life, King Charles VII retained his crown and ordered Joan of Arc to be formally innocent in 1456 by making her a martyr. She was canonized in the year 1920 and thus became France's patron saint. Most commonly, people seemed to think that she was insane and suffered from epilepsy. The Church, the army and the aristocracy were three central pillars of current society during the time of medieval Europe. Joan was really an outcast from these power spheres. She grew up in a family of farmers. But she could still negotiate in 1428 to induce the French Crown Prince, Charles of Valois, to evict the French English with a promise of prophecy that a virgin would come to save France. Following her death, Joan has become a symbol of belief without negotiation. Her memory continues to inspire women and committed Christians and military leaders throughout the world. The spiritual dreams of Joan d'Arc has been a continuing subject of discussion.

John Forbes Nash

(1928 - 2015) Mathematician

John Nash was a scientist and visionary. He had a far-reaching influence with his research, beginning with complex systems, market economics, sociology and evolutionary biology. Nash released his initial academic paper at the age of 17 together with his father He graduated from Princeton University in the USA, an institution packed of geniuses like Einstein. His tale is portrayed in the movie "A Beautiful Mind." He was admitted to mental treatment because of his conditions and remained in hospitals for almost 12 years. Nash went on to say he began to see delusional personalities who worked for an agency where everyone wore red ties.

Those were the ones who were constantly chasing him. The tale of Nash is like that of a good man with a lot of personal struggles. On his discharge from a hospital for paranoid schizophrenia treatment. He managed to make further progress in game theory, economics and market research. Upon emerging from mental asylum, he wrote almost 25 journal articles. He heard constant imaginary voices and had many strange ideas. To justify his concerns regarding aliens and also communists, he communicated with the Vatican, the UN and also with the FBI as he could identify them as they wore red ties. He also believed he received messages from space through the newspaper the New York Times. Nash wrote a letter which was preserved hidden from the public for 57 years by the US National Security Agency, in it he suggested the P=NP problem. This problem is one of the main unanswered questions in computer science. There is a reward, of 1 million dollars, waiting for anyone who can come up with a solution. He also introduced modern encryption in a formal way. It is believed that the Nobel Committee took very seriously his mental illness as they had obvious concerns that he might not behave appropriately before the King of Norway. After the ceremony, a dinner took place at Princeton University, but his only comments to the honour shown unto him was: "the cookies are better than usual today."

While his contributions included a large number of
fields of mathematical sciences, his research in the
advancement of game theory would probably be
the best of his legacy. In its purest form, game theory
is an analysis of conflicting models of cooperation
between decision-makers, and it is now a framework
for used throughout life sciences, which has led to
many major advancements both in evolutionary
biology and community behavior. Nash and his
girlfriend Alicia died in an accident during cab drive
in 2015.

John Harvey Kellogg

The most popular doctor of the early 20th centuries was possibly John Harvey Kellogg. In the Battle Creek Sanitarium, many patients like political leaders, corporate giants, and movie stars all were treated with enemas and underwent electrical currents to their eyes. The idea of consuming only clean food, practicing fitness and other natural remedies were treatments adopted by Dr. Kellogg. He was also the man who created cornflakes which were originally designed to prevent young boys from masturbating and not primarily as a breakfast meal. He was the man who promoted circumcision for young boys as punishment for the masturbation habits.

Or the use of carbonic acid explicitly to
a girl clitoris if they too played too much with their
private parts. He was also an advocate of stitching the
foreskin of boys, tying children's hands together, and
using electro-shock therapy and other special
machines that would make normal erections
excruciating. Kellogg has certainly anyway done good
for plenty of people. But he wasn't a great doctor, and
maybe not a good individual. Nothing was more
obvious than his fixation with the destructive
potential of masturbation habits. The real issue is that
Kellogg was very declarative without testing
alternative theories and without providing any real
proof of his conclusions. Kellogg declined to even
believe that he might indeed be wrong and offered no
whatsoever proof that he in fact was correct. There is
no evidence of any double-blind studies carried out on
cloves and their effects on children's sex drive. The
undisputed not all that negative reputation of John
Harvey Kellogg and his wish for healthcare reform
carried on even a century beyond after his time.   He
used carbolic acid to destroy children's flesh and they
realized they had sinned. Perhaps he felt he was just
doing the work of God. He did not quote
other research, trials, tests or scientific facts. He also
seems to have persuaded himself that he was outside
their need.

Dr. Kellogg was 91 years old at the time of his death, implying that he actually understood something vital regarding the secrets to staying healthy.

John Whiteside "Jack" Parsons

(1914 - 1952) Rocket engineer

While Jack Parsons, developer of the Jet Propulsion Laboratory (JPL), and the father of rocket science, was somewhat scarce from historical records, he was an enigma, to say the least. He stirred up demons and ancient gods and delved into the beauty of sex magic. He believed that he had no boundaries and could materialize energies as legit as the unbelievable science that he helped to establish. Parsons was a friend of other eccentric figures such as L. Ron Hubbard and the mythical Aleister Crowley.

Also, Howard Hughes was his boss at one
point while he also was a phone mate of Wernher Von
Braun. He was interested in black magic
and supernatural causes, because he believed that he
could use the power of alchemy to change the
weather. He was preoccupied with studying stuff
such as ghosts and poltergeists, he thus wanted to
create a new lover for himself out of thin air.
Indeed, he wanted to manifest an "elemental" such
that he could get a new wife, a the ritual
which required masturbating the sound of enchanted
music. Because these things all contributed to
a cocktail of sheer insanity, he was well known for not
being fully normal. He became quite wealthy as
his research talent into rocket science provided for
him. He purchased a huge property and opened it
to his sex-magical cult of sorts, it soon became a
hedonist's den. At day, he was indeed a rocket
scientist who worked for the government, but at night
he jumped out from his coffins, ate menstrual cakes
and attempted to create poltergeists in order to have
sex with them. The FBI was naturally a little
concerned, but they did not find any sign of a real
safety risk. Although his scientific career's academic
interest was trivial, historians have recognized
Parsons many contributions to modern rocket
engineering.

Parsons is hence regarded as one of the most prominent figures of the history of the US space program for his innovations, his outreach for space exploration as well as spaceflight. Parsons died in 1952 at the age of 37 in a domestic laboratory fire that brought attention to national media; the police deemed it as an incident.

Joseph Smith

(1805 - 1844) Religious leader

Mormonism may apply to many various groups while sometimes catching popular interest. The most famous of the Mormons is the Latter-day Saints Church of Jesus Christ, established in the early 1800s. In 1831, the known founder of the religion, Joseph Smith, got a prophecy that God ordered him to violate the current law and take himself many wives. With varied from ages at marriage, they were thus according to the faith eternally sealed unto him, they were between the ages of 56 and 14. The reality that Smith had widespread support of "plural marriage" does not come as a shock.

Scholars and various theologians have long debated his acceptance of the custom as a road to divine exaltation. As an institution in recent modern decades, the Mormon church has not been unable to undermine the unorthodox marital habits of its early founders. Many LDS church offshoots are seen as fundamentalist, polygamous churches. The church of the LDS does not trust or endorse this method. Joseph claimed that the Church of Christ was founded by Jesus himself, which had been suppressed during the Great Apostasy and which became a late revival of early Christian religion. Conservative Christians view God as a "necessary being" which implies that he cannot not in fact exist, and all other creatures are "conditional beings." To Mormonism, on the other side, both deity and human beings are just as important. Mormonism declares Christ to have been the firstborn Son of God, and his resurrection gave all men immortality Reports show Joseph Smith was confused regarding religion at the age of 14 as he went into the forest to pray. He asserted that both God and Jesus Christ decided to visit him in 1820, they told him that an angel named Moroni had buried some gold plates not so far from their farm which 14 centuries earlier he would find. The Angel said they included an ancient population record and the location from which they originated.

The Golden Plate story is a key part of the Mormon story, because in the view of many believers the discovery of this record and its translation of its content into the Book of Mormon validates Smith's belief that he was truly a Prophet sent by God. During the 19th century, almost every new leader of a religious organization was seen as being yet another nutcase by critics. Joseph was subsequently convicted by the Illinois government of treason and conspiracy and incarcerated alongside his own brother. The anti-Mormon crowd attacked and murdered the twins on in 1844. Joseph Smith's legacy is a combined worldwide congregation, of over 16 million adherents to the faith.

Judy Garland

(1922 - 1969) Actress, singer and vaudevillian

She was a symbol of entertainment as a film and music sensation from her young days. She was famous for her part in "The Wizard of Oz" and "A Star is Born." She was later recognized as the most accomplished actress of her time. Garland was also an outstanding singer and a Grammy award winner, while also being a popular actress. Despite her fantastic success, however, Garland's life was heart breaking, tainted by heavy drug abuse, suicidal patterns and failed relationships. At the age of 13, after meeting a film studio's co-founder, Garland was swiftly signed by MGM after an audition. Astonished by her lovely voice and singing, they did not need a screen test and recruited her right there. The studio acted severely and harshly against her during her employment. They monitored Garland's food consumption and worried about her weight. Nutrition were often withheld from her and she would become constantly hungry. For the remainder of her life, she would continue to be unconfident about herself image. Garland also had a postpartum depression, which saw her doctor giving her even more medication in addition to the medicines with which she was self-medicating. Garland was fired after 15 years by MGM, and she later had a nervous breakdown as she fell out of control, even trying to commit suicide a couple of times. Garland's success comprised of few erratic appearances at the end of her life before she died from an overdose of sedatives. Even though Garland endured that much, she did not let it influence how other people were treated by her. She continued to be a moral and financial support to different causes including the Civil Rights Movement. Garland has been commonly regarded as a sex symbol and referred to as "The Elvis of homosexuals." Many of Garland's friends were important people and prominent individuals in the LGBTQ community while she would also be seen often in gay bars with her homosexual friends.

Karl Emil Maximilian Weber

(1864 - 1920) Sociologist, philosopher, and political economist

Throughout his lifetime Weber's significance became essential among social scientists, some of whom also were his dear friends. Weber wrote countless essays and books during his lifetime. Considering how much he managed to write, the wide array of translations of content that he created, and the quantity written on Weber's theories by others, it is daunting to encounter this giant. As a thinker, Weber had the strongest merit of bringing social sciences into immediate critical standoff in Germany, which until then had been mainly concerned regarding national problems.

Together with the official titans of European thinking of the 19th century, Marx and Nietzche, by the very nature of this standoff, Weber helped establish a method and literature that took issue with topics like religion, political policy and social sciences. Max Weber experienced a major depressive downturn with repeated ailments in the subsequent years. In his research, Weber was intensely interested indirectly with the social, cultural and socioeconomic background of depressive encounter and behavior patterns. In 1895, his work the "Liberal imperialism" his extensive assault on German policies in World War I became widely debated, his thoughts energized a liberal attitude against the goals of war set out by the government, thus leading the leaders of the time to perceive Weber as domestic traitor. The essay is noteworthy for the manner in which Weber combined social theory and spiritual sociology, for the extent in which he explored and postulated the interaction between both the cultural domain of beliefs and values and the economic structure of society. Regarded as one of his main theoretical creations: his definition of the link between both culture and the economy, became the conceptualization of how individuals and institutions end up coming to have and accepted authority between them and how they maintain it.

Hence the "Iron cage" of any bureaucratic system as he saw it dictates how our lives are shaped. To Weber the interpretation of contemporary society as that of an iron cage, demonstrates society requires a large degree of individual compliance with the role of authority. Weber appears to suggest that the economic and technological interactions are structured and created by capitalist production which also implies they have become societal fundamental

forces themselves. Therefore, if a person is raised into such a culture, their existence and their view of the world is formed to such a degree that one cannot possibly even consider how a different form of living even feels like. Weber saw the iron cage as a massive obstacle to individual freedom. Weber's views on power and political inequality, which he communicated in his book "Economy and Society", spurred many sophisticated formulations from other people regarding social and cultural-economic status of individuals. The philosophical strategy of Weber must also attract understanding of psychopathological analysis of the structural traits of a depressed person. At the age of 56, Weber contracted Spanish influenza and died of pneumonia. Although his life was brief, his influence is strong and successful even today.

Karl Marx

(1818 - 1883) Philosopher, sociologist, political theorist

Karl Marx's achievements have persisted well after his murder on 14th of March 1883. His legacy concentrates on the lingering effects of sociology, politics and his economic theories. His supporters have also sought to define his works and to extend their assessments in the contemporary world to clarify how various social and economic phenomena affect us all and how it is possible to develop alternate solutions to the current socio-economic systems of most nations. The founder of classical Marxism, Karl Marx clearly left a lot of his ideas incomplete.

Classical Marxism appears to believe in a transformation called socialism, a stage between capitalism and communism, in contrast with anarchism that aims at establishing communism right after capitalism has been overthrown through revolution. Communism is an ideology engineered to establish a communist society that is stateless and, more than anything else, classless. Therefore, a communist society must be distinguished from the communist state commonly discussed in western political discourse. The latter is a socialist state controlled by a Communist Party. Marx launched radical ideas that examined modern economic and social order systems. His ideas were mainly disseminated via his written works now part of contemporary literature in sociology. What managed to make Marx a groundbreaking philosopher was his coherent assessment of the social order of his day. The ideas and principles he developed in the mid-1800s remain crucial structures for critical stance on the social and economic system of capitalism. Of course, Karl Marx's economic and political complex legacy is very challenging. It is reasonable to argue that the unsuccessful implementation of his classical Marxist ideas during the devastating, Soviet Union wars, the ineffective Great Leap Forward of China and during the Vietnam War has made him accountable for thousands of deaths in the mind of some people.

Marx suffered from poor conditions of health and as such many authors have tried to characterize and understand his suffering. Some have attributed this to problems of liver and gall, of which Marx was never symptom-free, and which were worsened by a lifestyle that was unreasonable. Sometimes he experienced headache attacks which occurred with nausea, swelling of his ear and rheumatic discomfort. A severe nervous condition arose in 1877 and he suffered from persistent insomnia triggered by opioids. The disease was amplified by increased night work and poor diet. His grave is engraved with quotations from Marx's own works such as the final lines of the "Communist Manifesto" which says: "'Workers from all lands unite." Marx complex theories extend Hegel's philosophical version of history. As shown by Hegel, the purpose of humanity is the deliverance of the human spirit, until we all realize that we are members of a universal human consciousness. Marx turned this "idealist" narrative into a "materialist" account in which the motivating factor of history is the affirmation of our basic citizen material needs, hence empowerment he saw as being achieved through class struggle. The working class would come to be the instrument for social emancipation through a rejection of private property.

Kurt Cobain

(1967 - 1994) Singer, composer, and musician

Kurt Cobain became famous as the leader of the legendary Nirvana rock band in the mid 1980s. While it initially looks as if he had a normal childhood, while he was nine years old, his parents divorced, causing him tremendous emotional pain. Cobain suffered greatly from extreme bronchitis and strenuous physical trouble due to an undiagnosed serious stomach disease most of his career, well before his newfound Nirvana popularity. He started to use drugs to deal with the pain and everything else going on in his life.

His use of drugs expanded to taking LSD, heroin, large amounts of alcohol and many other types of drug abuse. He also had depression and a long history of diverse mental illness, he also at times indeed was considering suicide, while depression ran through in his family. It is well-known that Kurt had been struggling with the publicity pressure and expectations of someone being labelled "the voice of a generation," few people have ever contradicted that he fit the description very well. He pivoted the stream of popular culture thru all the his truly amazing guitar playing, his musicianship, his public characters and even with his premature death. Nirvana had an extraordinary effect on the world of music for a group that produced only 3 studio albums. Theirs is the drive that moved alternative music into the mainstream away from the dark spots of university radios and small record shops. A swarm of other rockers, who tried to run through the nirvana door launched up to take their own chance at fame following their success. Kurt spoke out about the rights of gay people, irrational homophobia and rampent sexism. He claimed he only pretended to be homosexual, just so that he could offend homophobes, and even often wore clothing to oppose misogyny. He also permitted himself to tag cars with the words "God is gay", he was thus detained by the police on charges of graffiti.

Despite Nirvana's creation and Kurt's passing, it's easy to overlook that the icon was incredibly insightful and emotional. Cobain was discovered dead in his own home on 8 April 1994. He died by suicide of a self-inflicted gunshot wound to his head. The conditions surrounding the death of Kurt Cobain have given rise to considerable discussion and debates. The fact of the matter is that the life of Kurt Cobain has been diminished and he will persist influence future generations.

Kurt Gödel

(1906 - 1978) Logician and mathematician

Gödel indeed was a wonderful logician and a wise mathematician, also close friend of Albert Einstein. Einstein's human intelligence in contrast made him appear slightly peculiar and unusual to the average individual, but he seemed to have never suffered from any mental disorder. On the other side, Gödel figured somebody would kill him. He was so convinced of this misconception, particularly later on in life, that only food cooked by his wife would be deemed safe for him to eat, typically he first had to make her taste it. Hypochondriac health concerns became a chronic worry of his.

He was hospitalized for starvation multiple times. Through his philosophy, thoughts on logic and theology Gödel wrote several papers. Gödel attempted to solve the Continuum hypothesis. He made progress by demonstrating that the addition of certain axioms did not prove or refute the hypothesis. At 25 years old, Kurt Gödel had developed his famed "Incompleteness Theorems." His simple results revealed that there are ideas found in all consistent axiomatic systems that are cannot be confirmed or debunked within the system, and the validity of the axioms cannot be established. In contrast to its findings of formal number theory, thus Gödel documented evidence of a relative consistency of the choosing axiom and of the generalized hypothesis of continuum. His findings impacted strongly the finding that even a computer can actually never be designed to address all mathematical queries. His findings ended logical efforts like those of Bertrand Russell. But while Gödel was a perfect logician, he always thought somebody would kill him by intoxicating him. Gödel was an introvert as well. He would prevent touching with other people and his own body. In the year 2000, Gödel was included in TIME magazine as one of the top 100 most important thinkers. Gödel published data in formal logic, known to be vital characteristics of mathematics during the 20th century.

Indeed, Gödel proved that the vain hope of mathematics could not have been reduced to a simple axiomatic system, as earlier mathematicians and many philosophers previously had envisaged. Eventually, his digestive problems and particularly his reluctance to eat led to his death on 14 January 1978. He died at the age of 71.

Leo Tolstoy

(1828 - 1910) Writer and author

Leo Tolstoy indeed was a great author as a realistic disciple and one of the finest novelists in the world. Tolstoy was mainly known for his works, "War and Peace" and "Anna Karenina," these are also recognized as being two of the greatest ever published novels. Until early adulthood, Tolstoy didn't suffer from apparent symptoms of depression, however when it occurred, it hit very badly. He suffered severe personality swings and almost everything about his life was challenged by himself. Often, he mentioned giving everything away, all his belongings and he questioned even the essence of his religious faith.

At one juncture he was committed to giving up writing entirely and said, "Art is not only useless but even harmful." Hence Tolstoy is prime example of a person who apparently lost everything due to his disease which made all other things, the more, less important. Although he came from a rich family, was revered for his authorship and a father of 13 children, his demons nearly drove him to contemplate suicide sincerely. He was a very successful author, yet he still saw himself in retrospect as a refuge from his past glory behind him whenever he fell into a full-blown depression. In his own terms, the tragedy had pulled him far enough to even take away his strength for suicide, the condition that is not uncommon with people with serious periods of depression. Tolstoy indeed worked very hard, suffered greatly and lived a full life while still trying to find a true sense to his purpose, perhaps because of his spiritual awakening. Tolstoy also became world acclaimed as a religious and moral teacher, particularly during the late stages of his life. His philosophy of non-resistance and pacifism against evil inspired such men as Gandhi greatly. Although the beliefs of Tolstoy no longer gain the reverence as they once were well known, interest in his character and personality has grown over the years.

Among the people who met him it was common to
describe him as godly in his abilities and a great
icon in his efforts to evade the constraints of the
human condition. Some saw Tolstoy as personification
of nature as well as purity of life, while others
viewed him as the epitome of a world conscience. He
truly was not only on of the best writers, but also
a sign of the quest for knowledge and purpose of life.

Leonardo Da Vinci

(1452 - 1519) Renaissance polymath

Notwithstanding his greatness in anything from scientific knowledge and music to literature, sculptures and of course, artwork. Yet to himself he was as a failure. His customers frequently were not very kind to him either, by many accounts thinking of him as being frustrating and not at all reliable. Historical documents show that Da Vinci invested too much time preparing activities but did not actually persevere to carry them out. ADHD might explain the disposition of Leonardo and his odd temperamental genius.

The efficiency of Da Vinci implicated extended periods of lazy downturns, intermixed with periods of extreme creativity, sometimes prompted by the vicinity of a more settled worker. His imaginative productions were at times largely overshadowed by customers and associates who became frustrated about the low, sluggish completion percentage of the artist. Da Vinci had not been a big fan of sleeping. The Polyphasic Cycle of the Italian Renaissance genius saw him taking only power naps approximately every 24 hours. Thomas Edison was another follower of this form of relaxation, as Da Vinci's fellow scientist, he too is one who could justify how they both had accomplished so much with so little sleep. While he is best remembered as more of an artist, the engineers which was Leonardo has created some incredible inventions. Leonardo developed mechanical contraptions which are in use even unto this day, from the early draft of the aircraft to a primeval diving suit. However, Leonardo was just not your ordinary inventor. He didn't have any formal education, disassembled anything and even animals, and he loved the design of war machines. In the meantime, particularly in comparison to the exposure that artists get these days, Da Vinci's work had never been publicly or critically validated during his lifetime.

As such that actually seemed to have died complaining that he had offended mankind and God himself because he felt himself that he had not worked hard enough. As can be seen by acknowledgement, he still successfully designed the initial heart valve, created designs for robots and even for digital computers. We currently resonate Leonardo as an artist who pioneered the Renaissance art, but he was praised by his peers as a research scientist whose striking inventions resulted in a new era as he created a different way of thinking. Da Vinci died of a possible stroke at the age of 67, in 1519. He kept working on his scientific research all the time up until his death. Many of us today know the famous creations of Leonardo. Leonardo's works of art have been the cutting edge of our historical cultural memory, ranging from the "Last Supper" to the "Vitruvian Man," and of course the famous "Mona Lisa."

King Ludwig II

(1845 - 1886) King of Bavaria

Without Ludwig, perhaps the worst of all of them, no royal eccentrics list is complete. His mother was worried when he succeeded to his throne that he was really not mentally fit enough to rule Bavaria. Ludwig had almost no political interest, no military involvement or any of a monarch's ordinary concerns. Instead he had an artistic curiosity and also had a keen interest in Richard Wagner's music.

He welcomed Wagner to Bavaria where Wagner's operas were turned into shrines in Bayreuth and, in his gradual retirement from public life, Ludwig dedicated himself to the arts. A trip to France showed him how the French had restored their Renaissance and Medieval monuments and that it was necessary to re-establish Bavaria's architecture; otherwise he would construct them and there would be no other chateaux to be restored. In his cherished fairytale buildings, such as Schloss Neuschwanstein, he invested wonderfully, it later also became Walt Disney's model of for his castles. The growth of Prussia and his victorious war between Austria and France shook Ludwig back to reality. A powerful Catholic, King Ludwig originally supported Austria, but in the French-Prussian War he nudged after Bismarck. Free status of the numerous smaller domestic states of the German land practically ended with the establishment of the German Empire, but Ludwig persisted as king of partially independent Bavaria. His conduct, nevertheless, was deeply worrying for his officials. He cancelled his wedding plans, most likely on account of his homosexuality and spent money on his cherished castles more and more until his officials felt obliged to act. Several physicians were able to assert Ludwig as being insane and, therefore, unable to govern, because many of them had not met him, even fewer had evaluated him.

When Ludwig showed up in the palace, Bavarian authorities deployed to detain him. Nevertheless, Ludwig was removed from office and imprisoned in the neighboring mansion, where he was later found dead in conditions which were never adequately explained.

Ludwig van Beethoven

(1770 - 1827) Classical and romantic composer

Beethoven was a guy who was susceptible to emotional extremes. He would have been totally depressed and drowned in alcohol in his sadness for a moment and would be full of enthusiasm and joy in the next moment. Beethoven had been raised by an abusive father, who attempted seeing him as a child prodigy and to exploit him. While he composed only 9 symphonies, as a child Beethoven began to learn music at a young age with his dad who taught him piano and violin, he played for the first time in public when he was six.

Throughout his social circle, Beethoven's episodes of mania were very well recognized and, when he was on a high note, he would write several works at once. Some of his most famous plays were published during his mental down times. Unfortunately, he thought about suicide too, this is known as his brothers were informed in letters during his lifetime. In the beginning of 1813, he was so depressed that he stopped thinking about his looks and went into rage at dinner parties. During his twenties he even started losing his hearing and by the age of 40 he was already altogether deaf. It must have made the situation miserable for a composer. He just almost pretty much stopped writing throughout that period. Just as the composer passed away of liver failure, he must have self-medicated with drinking for decades to tackle his many health issues. The autopsy at the end of his life showed that excessive alcohol use was caused his weakened liver. Unfortunately, everything that he actually suffered from would have been treatable with today's drugs, including a severe case of bipolar disorder. Beethoven is among the most famous composers of the Classical Era, however his dominance is much more profound. While transforming music from conventional classical style to Romanticism, Beethoven played a key role while his individual expression became even more known.

Without such influence of talented composers such as Beethoven, the world wouldn't enjoy what contemporary music is today. It's been said about him, that Beethoven developed the common idea of the "artist" as an individual with a deep impact on culture, isolated from society. Approximately 20,000 Viennese residents went to his funeral, a clear indication of the impact he had on his peers and the public.

Ludwig Boltzmann

A life defined by: $S=\kappa\cdot\log W$? The formula is a rather nerdy inscription on the grave of the physicist and founder in statistical mechanics, Ludwig Boltzmann. The equation shows the relationship regarding entropy as well as the probability of thermodynamic state of activity of all matter. It contains a constant later called after Boltzmann. Boltzmann had been a contemporary of the well-known Georg Cantor, the guy who was trying to define infinity and solve the Continuum Hypothesis by manage to throw the entire field of math into uncertainty.

While Charles Darwin released his "Origin of Species," Boltzmann was just 15 years old. Science was shaken from across all sides of thought, the framework of a divine intelligent design worldview was no more because of its defined boundaries and limits which now were torn down. Never would the world and science be the same again. Boltzmann studied Physics and obtained his PhD for his research on the Kinetic Theory of Gases at the University of Vienna. At the moment, it was highly contentious that the passage of tiny objects-atoms and molecules, should determine the characteristics of materials. The key factor of thermodynamics is that entropy becomes inevitable and almost always is increasing, rendering decay probable and relentless in all matter. And, in brief, the condition of disorder is that which we are headed for is always presumed as such to be higher in the coming future. Balance is therefore dictated from within, not from outside, the atoms, positions and behavior determine the future of all things. During his life, many had been worried about Boltzmann's mental health, with excesses of manic behavior and wild passion and phases of serious depression indicated what would be in today's term a bipolar disorder. He was also admitted to the hospital for depression several times. His anxiety might also have been due to his unsuccessful persistence in supporting his own ideas.

Boltzmann also was reported to have asthma and poor vision. The discomfort that these limitations caused him, could also be the source of his heavy anxiety. He hanged himself just 4 months after another failed suicide attempt related to his ill health and anxiety without even leaving a note. Boltzmann's observation, with the assistance of Max Planck as well as Albert Einstein, achieved its merited success and recognition among scientists after his death. The legacy of Boltzmann is among the most prominent and inspirational of all the fantastic physicists and mathematicians during the 19th century. His advances of statistical mechanics have shown how the principles of microscopic physics could explain macroscopic processes, a genuine victory and fulfillment of the mechanistic worldview paradigm.

Ludwig Wittgenstein

(1889 – 1951) Philosopher

Wittgenstein has introduced to contemporary philosophy many pioneering works, primarily on the basis of logic, mathematical theories, language theory and philosophy of mind. He is a key person in the construction of analytical philosophy in both his older and newer works: he expects us to see that use of natural speech is essential for understanding the nuances of our mind.

While Wittgenstein himself did not dispute that we still have individual experiences such as pain, suffering or guilt, which we term cognitive and psychological conditions, he claimed we interpret all of them by our words. In his family, several others committed suicide, among them one of Ludwig Wittgenstein's cousins and sadly also three of four brothers Wittgenstein also himself considered suicidal sentiments throughout his life starting from his early teens. Wittgenstein experienced severe depression through his years as a teacher in Austria. His observations on cognitive theory were to Wittgenstein at that period without much value, yet they later had a tremendous influence on existentialist philosophy and psychology. For instance, he once asserted that every existential suggestion was in fact nonsensical or meaningless. Although he rejected the Marxist theory, Wittgenstein still identified himself as a Communist, as such romanticizing the lives of workers. Wittgenstein thoughts would change throughout the course of time, such as his philosophical views, his religious faith in Christianity, for which he often publicly declared a genuine and committed sympathy for. In a letter Wittgenstein stated that Mozart as well as Beethoven in fact were God's actual sons. Wittgenstein's had intimate relations with both women and men. He is assumed to have fallen in love three times with other men.

Wittgenstein's sexuality also sparked a lot of distress in him leading to self-doubt about his homosexual desires. Wittgenstein's sexual urges has somehow tarnished the monastic moral imperative which has been developed towards him as a philosopher. It was indeed a major problem for many when trying to understand him. Nonetheless, various thinkers in the school of analytics will continue to consider him as one of the most influential and important thinkers of the 20th century. He worked until he died from prostate cancer in Cambridge in 1951.

Mahatma Gandhi

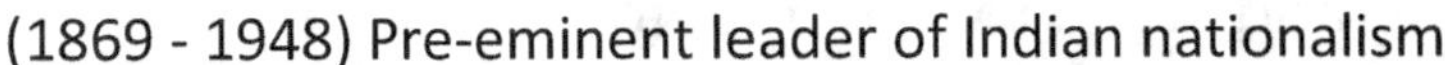

(1869 - 1948) Pre-eminent leader of Indian nationalism

Gandhi was not given the name of "Mahatma" meaning "great soul" as India knew him as, until 1914, once he had established a credibility as an attorney and social activist, he later became known as the "father of the nation". He was a shrewd political activist who struggled for the freedom of India against British rule as well as for the rights of all people especially poor Indians. His model of non-violent protest has become admired worldwide and still inspires many today. Within Mahatma Gandhi's memoir of 1948, it is stated that he attempted to kill himself as a young man.

Distracted by the British Empire towards India's subjugation, Gandhi and a companion obtained poison and came to a temple to execute their own suicide. During the last minute, however they failed to make a decision and only drank a non-lethal dose. This first event in Gandhi's life was accompanied by a further series of different periods of depression and extreme anxiety. He was incarcerated for many years in both South Africa and in India on numerous occasions. In 1915 he moved back to India from South Africa at the age of 45. In demonstration against disproportionate land taxation and prejudice, he organized farmers, peasants and urban workers to fight for the cause. In 1921, as president of the Indian National Congress, Gandhi headed national attempts to alleviate poverty, extend women's rights, establish religious and racial unity, eliminate caste system and, above all, accomplish Swaraj or self-government. His ideology finally led India to become independent from Britain in 1947. Even though Gandhi was eventually assassinated by a Hindu fundamentalist months later, the murderer opposed Gandhi's notion of secular democracy in India. Gandhi is known as one of the world's greatest idealists. By his work, he affected people's lives not only in India, but throughout the world. He trusted in icons such as Martin Luther King Jr and Nelson Mandela.

Of course Gandhi and King did manage with success to a certain degree but they also in part did fail: India was deeply split since Hindus and Muslims couldn't really tolerate each other, and in the US segregation finally ended, albeit painfully and at the cost of much cultural and social damage, effects which still felt today. Radical empathy politics finally proved to be outside the ability of the ordinary, mentally normal and healthy public.

Mao Zedong

(1893 - 1976) Chairman of the Communist Party of China

Mao was a Communist figure and the People's Republic of China's leader. He was in charge of the destructive policies of the "Great Leap Forward" and the "Cultural Revolution." Mao mostly seemed to be pushing towards his desire to attain power. He followed his goals for much of his adult lives with unabated passion and persistence and discarded himself of anyone, even relatives and genuine friends if they were not able to further his objectives. Mao is liable in varying levels of the killing of millions of people, much more than Hitler or even Stalin are credited for. It is a story of torture, brutality, bewilderment and outrageous human devastation.

Mao was intrigued with fear and violence from a very early age, but he was most fascinated in how terror and murder were being used to obtain power. Some of his favorite ways to strike fear and panic through paranoia was to get individuals to start accusing someone else of being a counter-revolutionary. Mao did not want anybody to be killed for being a counter-revolutionary except if they were trying to undermine his interests. Mao demanded that the farmers raise their grain production and then obtained the bulk of this surplus to bargain for weapons from Russia. He caused widespread starvation at a rate unparalleled in worlds history, with 30 million reported deaths which was insignificant to Mao, his fixations eventually gave him his powerhouse. The People's Republic of China, declared itself socialist, characterized by a unique form of their own later embrace of capitalism. The real definition of socialism is a society in which the means of production, distribution and exchange are owned not by private individuals but by the community as a whole. Socialism, thus in fact, is an ideology which tries to achieve this type of society. Later, he became mentally disintegrated. It thus was towards the very last part of his constant struggle as a Nationalist dictator who sobbed whenever he talked about the objectives which he had not achieved.

Mao had as reported by several accounts, severe personality disorders, including narcissistic and paranoid personality disorder. He was also very satisfied through his tendency to carry out brutal violence. His dream of China represented this strong psychopathological explicitly. As "schadenfreude" was a recurrent impulse on his way to the top, self-pity took hold of him during his last decades of spiteful dissatisfaction. Following years of poor health, he suffered of heart attacks and died at the age of 82. In China, both the rich and poor, the young and old, still look at him as a spiritual guide who stood up against foreign imperial forces and ended a hundred years of indignity.

Marcus Tullius Cicero

(106 - 43 BC) Roman lawyer, orator, philosopher and statesman

The Roman attorney, speaker, politician, and thinker of whom we are well conscious more than any other Roman Citizen, Cicero lived through both the agitating period of Julius Caesar's emergence, his enduring tyranny, and his ultimate demise. Cicero had been sent to get his education in Rome. He studied music, mathematics and fundamental principles of rhetoric when he was just 14. He later also began studying literature, politics and philosophy. His political discourses and his communications show the enthusiasm, friction and suspense of politics and his role in the time of turmoil. Of the estimated 106 addresses given by him to the Roman citizens, of them only 58 exist today.

Cicero provided his very own philosophy and was an unmatched interpreter who turned Greek ideas in to incisive Latin. His certain unparalleled achievement was seen through his letters. Over 900 of his correspondence still exist of this day, from government intercepts to personal messages to family and friends. Most of what is understood about history and his era's culture is established by the letters from Cicero. But none of his writings became prepared for print, but Cicero allowed his joys, worries and grievances full reign of thoughts in his writing. In the writings, messages and dialogs of Cicero, he became regarded as the finest orator of the Roman Republic. A wonderful lawyer and his family's first to get into Roman office. Although Cicero did appear to have suffered from anxiety and lack of conviction, it clearly did not stop him from considering complex legal situations at a young age. Cicero was assassinated in 43 B.C.E., by the instruction of his competitor Mark Antony, due to his hatred of Cicero for having supported the assassination of Caesar indirectly. His death could not mute the legislator whose remarks had been read, heard and even committed to memory for millennia by later Western leaders. Over the generations, Cicero's writings have barely diminished in impact.

By him the Renaissance and Enlightenment philosophers explored the abundance of traditional rhetoric and diverse philosophy of early era.

Marilyn Monroe

(1926 - 1972) Actress, model, and singer

Marilyn Monroe was a creation, it's no secret. Born as Norma Jeane Mortenson, the young actress grew up poorly and mainly in various foster care homes, only to modify her name and also her hair color in order to reach a fame level which nobody can possibly match. Her statuesque appearance and blonde hair style make it easy even for people that know next to nothing about film to notice her. Indeed, she was symbol of international elegance, mystique and sexual legendry. She had a difficult childhood, including undependable parents who never quite looked after their daughter. Marilyn's mother actually stayed in mental institutions for several times whereas her father left the family.

Family members have confirmed that Marilyn has had delusional hallucinations and paranoia as a kid, such as the episode involving her dog's death. Marilyn had trouble relating at school with other kids, but at least she had a close connection with her pet, Tippy. One day, while Marilyn's was in class, a car hit Tippy. A neighbor found the dog and put him in Marilyn's house driveway. Tippy was apparently struck by a car, but later Marilyn refused to acknowledge the account. She became firmly convinced that the neighbor, who protested about the noise of the dog, brutally murdered him by slicing pet into two with their garden tool. Nobody else could persuade her. The accident involved Marilyn's caregivers Ida and Wayne Bolender. Despite the challenges she encountered as a foster child, Marilyn developed and progressed towards a future in Hollywood. Even so, in the rising star the symptoms of mental illness still were present. Fatigue, anxiety, depression and popularity continued to overwhelm Marilyn over the years. She would also suffer the pain of broken marriages and at certain three miscarriages. Monroe died of a "probable suicide" in 1962, the medical examiner eventually said that the manner of death was an "acute barbiturate poisoning,"

Few celebrities have provided such a strong legacy to the world despite such a brief life and sad outcome. Marilyn Monroe has become the focus of many movies, plays, books and tv shows in the decades after her heyday, all of which are attempting to explain her popularity. Other actors have tried to capture her character, but in Showbiz history, Marilyn has always had a unique role, she will always persist as a truly unique Hollywood star.

Mark Twain

(1835 - 1910) Author and humorist

Twain was closely linked to Presidents, Royalty, business titans and musicians. Twain won the respect of his peers and detractors for his satirical writing, through which he considered America as a humourist of his day as he made fun of real societal problems. Even though Twain was considered among the most wonderful literary minds, he also sadly had bipolar disorder as well as other mental health issues. His most impressive work, "Huckleberry Finn" could even have been grounded in his propensity to depression. His curiosity in technology and innovation guided him to encounter Nikola Tesla as well as Thomas Edison.

He himself had three patents to his name upon his death. Twain was not the only Anglo-American to contend with all of the complexities of the issues of racial issues, but he remained a pioneering voice of race and slavery. He and his wife had lost their infant son to diphtheria and his beloved daughter died of spinal meningitis at the age of 24. His younger daughter had substantial condition of epilepsy. At the age of she eventually died of a heart attack. He had also been allegedly very depressed when his wife died. For his time, Twain remained an exceptionally dynamic author. Twain has always been known as a humorist, but he's much more, a social moralist, successful performer, political philosopher and novelist. He is indeed one of the world's leading influencers, traveling abroad, including a popular lecture tour hich he undertook around the world in which after conducted enabled him to get rid of his debts. His enormous autobiography was to be published 100 years after his death, as per his wishes. The story came out in 2010, finishing the unique distinction of being a bestselling author who in three separate decades has written new material. In his later years, Twain endured tectonic rages and fits of paranoia and suffered several episodes of depression. In 1910 Mark Twain eventually died of a heart attack at the age of 74.

Martin Luther

(1483 - 1586) Saxon priest, monk and theologian

Luther insisted that normal people had the same equal rights to God as Him. He thought that we should no more be denied the opportunity to worship or to study the Bible. People were on an equal footing with clergy and the nobles in God's sight and therefore deserves to be treated in similar fashion. Obviously, such a progressive perspective gained a lot of attention during that period of time. Many of the speeches of Luther were published and widely spread, and his texts proceeded to pervade a-growing field of attention.

The insight that redemption and mercy are gifts and cannot be earned, and also that the ordinary people are as absolutely correct and have as much full rights to God as clergy and nobles, reached over and above government at the time. For publishing houses, it was basically as printing cash when they distributed anything authored by Luther. Although we don't understand the first time Luther has been characterized by depression, it is known that he suffered at the time when he was a monk. Indeed, Luther has been well known and sometimes even ridiculed for his confessional rigor. After he entered the confessional, he checked his heart for fresh crimes that he had done or overlooked and refused to confess. It was a trial of his brethren priests who were stuck during these long sessions in the confessional with the monk Luther. Luther regularly flapped himself among meetings as well as in the tradition of times to show his remorse and to become closer to the nature of God. Sometimes these self-inflicted whippings were so severe that he drew blood. Revelation brought about an enormous transformation of Luther's spirit and pushed him into what many suffering, of bipolar disorders might identify as a manic state where he hyper-focused himself on the Bible, seeking for certain indications of his accuracy.

Through his writings, Max Weber claims that capitalism has grown to the advanced level of its development in the West, because Protestantism promoted labor to be taken up as a request from God and therefore a commitment to work permitted one to make much money. Coupled with quality of asceticism, living a pure physical life without lavish costly delights, this encouraged an egocentric yet cash hording mentality. Earlier, while the social influence of religion was diminishing, Weber claimed that capitalism was freed and developed as an economic accumulation process away from the limits set by Lutheran morality. With the philosophy of Protestantism in mind, Luther was known for writing for days with unbelievable productivity. Luther was given the death penalty for his work, he was constantly at odds even with his colleagues and continued writing, ranting, and even translating the Bible into German which became the very first translation into such a common language. Luther died in 1546 from natural causes. Yet his message started to spread, and his adherents took up the cause. Today's many modifications to theology triggered by his presence are taken for granted and some don't even refer to Luther.

Martin Luther King, Jr.

A Martin Luther King, Jr., was a Baptist minister and social activist who took the leading role in the American campaign for Civil Rights during the mid-1950s. For African Americans, as economically disadvantaged people and victims of inequality, King pursued racial equality through peaceful demonstration. He was the guiding force behind activities that led to groundbreaking laws such as the Civil Rights Act and also the Voting Rights Act. Martin Luther King, Jr. organized the March on Washington for Jobs and Freedom, a nonviolent rally intended to shed new light on the inequalities African Americans had to face throughout the country.

The march was attended by around approximately 300,000 people, and as he was stood at the steps of the Memorial of Lincoln, a president monument for the man that had demolished the slave institution in the United States a century earlier, the occasion ultimately resulted in King's most famous speech, known as the "I Have a Dream" address. A more committed and charismatic figure is hard to find then Martin Luther King, Jr. However, King struggled during his dark times. After two recorded suicide attempts, the civil rights activist experienced serious episodes of depression well into his adult life. His colleagues encouraged him to pursue psychiatric treatment, including after his rise to power as a human rights activist. Martin Luther King, Jr. was the first person to win the Nobel Peace Prize at the young age of thirty-five. After his selection was notified, he declared that he would donate the prize money to the support of the civil rights movement. Martin Luther King was killed on the night of 4 April 1968. Following his death, a barrage of riots swept through major cities around the country and a national day of mourning was declared by President Johnson. Martin Luther King Jr. devoted his life in the United States to the nonviolent battle against racial inequality and will forever be remembered as a true hero.

Michael Jackson

(1958 - 2009) Singer, songwriter and dancer

He is known as the "King of Pop," one of the most important cultural figures and as one of the biggest celebrities in the 20th century. Jackson's many great contributions to modern music, dance and fashion, as well as his public life, rendered him a worldwide known celebrity in contemporary culture. Jackson pioneered concert and music videos. A new era of music video was initiated by him, captivating fans with special effects such as "Thriller," "Black or white" and "Scream." Jackson was among the first celebrities in the world to start his own charity foundation.

His dedication to social justice has often been the focus of his art. Jackson made a notion of peace and collective responsibility a common ethos through his music. Millions and millions of fans worldwide once found his music's gravitation indisputable; today, it is possible that it's no less attracting than it ever was. Furthermore, his career lasted four decades, he sold approximately 750 million records around the globe and earned 13 Grammy Awards. The news, superficial, cynical and simplistic, fascinated Michael Jackson all through his career, but fell to miserable moral levels when the claims of abusive behavior against him were made public. In its most repulsive instance of media trials, reporters used the quirkiness of Michael to demonstrate his culpability over and over, and they were also soundly defeated by a jury decision of his contemporaries that at last managed to clear his name with an innocent verdict. Michael Jackson has remained in the entertainment business for years, while many of his peers have long ago fallen away from the same scene. Glancing at the life of Michael, we see several truths shouting out to be noticed and recognized. Financial difficulties, damaged relationships, dysmorphic bodily disorders and innumerable cosmetic operations, substance abuse and, if not criminal, peripheral relationships with some minors.

The reports of Jackson's death went viral quickly and people began to react globally and lament the sudden loss of the King of Pop Music. Jackson died due to an overdose administered by his doctor. Unlike his career, the demise of Michael Jackson overshadowed news bulletins worldwide in 2009 with an effect that lasted for years. Jackson memory is still plagued by contention even in death. Her idiosyncrasies and charges of sexual abuse remain a cause of circus and public discussion. Jackson's Wikipedia page is the second most edited, second only after Jesus. The people of the world reflect the ferocity by which the wide public wants to examine Jackson's story.

Michael Servetus

(1511–1553) Physician and theologian

Typically identified as Servetus, he was a Spanish physician theologian, cartographer and honest humanist. His skills included many fields; he published scientific works on celestial, meteorological, geological, physiological as well as medical treatises and poems. In 1545 he identified the lower circulation (pulmonary circulation). Since he wrote a book which included some observations on the reform of Christianity, the work was considered as heretical. Servetus wasn't really a skeptic religious.

When we bring it into a historical context, it becomes clear that Servetus is the main figure in the world who started the journey to recovery of the social humanistic framework. The Greco-Roman society of pre-Christianity era had enjoyed tolerance of religious, conscience and thinking freedom. The early Western society had no idea of the concept of "heresy" or even "heretics." Greco-Roman civilization accepted all faiths and placed no limits on expression of free thought. Acts of prejudice were uncommon and if they happened, divergences from one philosophy or another were not really justified as being wrong as such. This had been so due to the absence of any government or state religion because citizens within the power structures were also themselves religious. All of that has changed significantly with the emergence of Christianity supported by the state. Christianity had been an institution of within a centralized clergy system since the fourth century and was thus associated with political authority in the Roman Empire and subsequently in Western Europe. Just because Catholicism developed into a hierarchical totalitarian theocracy did it in fact prevail. He fled the Catholic Church and from Spain, but the Catholic Inquisition finally arrested him in Switzerland.

The uncompromising Catholic officials and Calvinists at Vienne and Geneva could not accept the resistance of the scientifically literate Servetus against their respective doctrines. Instead of coping rationally with his critical claims, Servetus was seized, beaten, and burnt alive amid copies of his book on the coast near Geneva, thus rendering Michael Servetus a genuine martyr of knowledge. Servetus positioned great significance on human natural improvisation, rationality and the capacity for good deeds, emphasizing human dignity and their independence in all moral choices. Servetus gave integrity and fair ability to identify good and evil to all people. Servetus is the first contemporary Christian philosopher to make clear the freedom of every citizen to obey their own convictions and to articulate their own judgments. He was also the first to suggest that persecuting or suppressing ideas was an offense.

Michel Foucault

(1926 – 1984) Philosopher

The entire work of Foucault is seen as inter-disciplinary by definition, covering fields of history, psychology, sociology and philosophy. Foucault`s critical theory rejects statements like fundamental scientific truths regarding human nature which, as shown by him, mostly simply manifestations of a given society's ethical as well as political engagement, demonstrating that they are still only the product of subjective historical powers, not scientifically sound realities. From an endless resentment of bourgeois society and past culture,

Foucault started out with a purposeful compassion for marginalized groups like madmen, homosexuals and convicted criminals. His obsession with power dynamics and the advancement of excluding narratives and repression in the area of mental health institutions caused some academics to view Foucault as a for of anti-psychiatrist. Foucault's analysis of how authority and expertise are essential for the mechanism by which humans are "rendered subjects" and therefore how psychological personalities are formed, denounces and reconstructs the theoretical basis and related medical and therapeutic procedures of mental and psychiatric care. The implication that Michel Foucault was homosexual in comparison is seriously contemplated to have influenced his perspective and work, yet still he is nevertheless praised for that. It was a very important part of his genealogy studies of the sexual history and tinted his vision of the sexuality of women. The analysis of Foucault on power was usually meant to diminish the role of the government in the public relations environment. In this situation, Foucault spins the word "governmentality," which has a very varying significance.

The role, of the concept of governmentality, would be to concentrate on states themselves as such, rather than the whole system or the environment of human culture when talking about diverse contemporary societies. The concept of government like that of power for Foucault, correlates with the difference between the state workmanship commonly known as "goverment" today and personal behavior, known as "self-government." This mindset however brings Foucault directly on the path of Ancient Greek ethics unto the Aristotelian basis where ruling others, relies on your relation as an individual to yourself. In particular, Foucault's thesis may be described as historical research focused on philosophy; towards to the end of his career, Foucault claimed that all his research was part of a greater effort to objectively explore the creation of truth. Foucault passed in Paris on 25 June 1984 as an apparent victim of AIDS. Not only did he heavily influence ethics and philosophy, but he also a provided insight into many fields of humanistic and social sciences. At the untimely time of his death, Foucault was alleged to be France's most prominent intellectual.

Michelangelo

Michelangelo was the most talented artist of the Italian Renaissance period, an artist, sculptor, builder and writer. Current research published in academic journals or elsewhere indicate that Michelangelo had both an obsessive-compulsive disorder as well as a high-functioning autism disorder or so namely Asperger syndrome. Throughout this context, you may have questioned how anybody could create anything as massive as the art seen on the Sistine Chapel's ceiling.

Of his peers, descriptions regarding the artist was that he was very concerned about his own reality. Most of his family's males are reported to have shown severe symptoms as well. He also may well have had problems in establishing relationships with other people; he had very few friends, and he did not even attend the funeral of his brother. All this coupled with his apparent talent for mathematics and art has prompted scholars to conclude that Michelangelo, is considered simply to be profoundly autistic. His painting on the Sistine Chapel where God creates Adam is still the most famous screensaver of all time. The outcome is a metaphysical example of how High Renaissance art incorporating Christianity's iconography and prophecy were among the fields of knowledge that Michelangelo absorbed in his childhood. Notwithstanding his status as one of the most famous painters in history, he had little regard for painting as a tool and interacted with other crafts, such as sculpture for example "The Statue of David" and extraordinary architecture of "St. Peter's Basilica." Even the most fundamental self-maintenance tasks were by Michelangelo totally ignored. Not just did he bathe very seldom, he never even changed his appearance and slept dressed, shoes also included.

And it was indeed his autism which really allowed him to concentrate compulsively on his work, as such sacrificing all else in his daily existence. It was the form of autism which helped him in his profession towards becoming famous worldwide. On February 18, 1564, only few weeks until his 89th birthday, Michelangelo died in Rome in the aftermath of a short disease. After his death, people respected him as the "father and master of all arts." Unlike some other artists, throughout his career, Michelangelo gained both fame and true wealth. He was also distinguished by having lived seeing the publishing of two biographies regarding his life. The admiration of the technical excellence of Michelangelo has persisted over centuries and his reputation has become associated with that of the finest Renaissance heritage.

Prophet Muhammad

The growth of Islam is connected inherently to Prophet Muhammad, who Muslims consider to be the very last in a long string of prophets, in which Moses and Jesus are included. While Muhammad was considered to be the appointed receiver or interpreter of the words of God only through his divine revelation, Muhammad started to have dreams and hearing voices when he was around forty years old. He sometimes would meditate on a hill near Mecca in pursuit for understanding.

The Archangel Gabriel came to him on one of these moments, and commanded him to say "in the name of your Lord." It was just one of many teachings to be the basis of the Quran, the religious text of Islam. Prophet Muhammad continued to receive these divine teachings over the ensuing 23 years. Such revelations, as the Quran, were eventually compiled and registered into one single book. Those initial revelations revealed the presence of one Deity, which was in contrast to the polytheistic teachings of the pre-Islamic Peninsula of Arabia. Upon his death, Muhammad did not appoint a successor. The Islamic faith is hence split between Sunni and Shia groups today. The discord among these two groups has led to both religious and political discrepancies. The majority of Sunnis occupy the Muslim world of today, with Shia concentrated in Iran and Iraq and elsewhere throughout the middle east. For his unjustified interpretation of scriptural passages in the Bible and its characters and for declaring himself as the last prophet, yet not performing any miracles, he was thus given the degrading title of "Ha-Meshuggah" by his fellow men. This was due to him not demonstrating some particular necessity requested in the Hebrew Bible of prophets and was thus called "The Madman" and "The Possessed."

Mainstream religious and hateful critique of Islam are issued towards Muhammad for stating himself to be a prophet, against his morality, his slave ownership, his hostile treatment of enemies, his marriages and his psychological condition. Muhammad was also accused of sadism and sexual relations with slaves and condemned for his marriage to an adolescent girl. Although Muhammad has been venerated as the Islamic Prophet, he was only a man who quickly told his supporters not to do wrong by worshiping him instead of the One God whom he preached about. In addition, Prophet Muhammad promoted the values of religious justice among all people regardless of race, gender, economic or social class. The Spiritual leader of Islam is unquestionably perceived throughout the world as being a great influence for mankind. Today around the whole earth, there are almost two billion Muslims who practice his lessons carefully and believe in the same God he advocated during his life.

Napoleon Bonaparte

(1769 - 1821) Military leader and politician

The French political figurehead and military commander Napoleon Bonaparte is an iconic figure of the past. His policies and actions had a major effect on European politics during the 19th century. Napoleon was recognized throughout his life for his intellect and charismatic personality. He was at that time praised by his teachers for his mathematics implementation in real life. He also had good insight in both geography and history. During his adulthood he displayed his intellect by adapting it towards his complex military strategies. He carefully orchestrated his actions which earned him several achievements.

Napoleon's surge into notoriety and honor during the first Republic of France was often depicted of him as being a tough-hearted individual. The rare organizational skills of Napoleon, as implemented to the Civil Code are justifiably considered of him as a great modernizer, although not as much regards to the particular issues of his warfare and rule of a totalitarian state with its most adventurous use of fear mongering. Accounts characterize his shortcomings as a statesman: he was not a moderate, often negligent of the life and needs of his own troops, he had indeed no external foreign policy other than warfare, he thus destroyed the revolution's moral veneration, and alienated even his own early supporters. Napoleon was indeed cavalier regarding his military victims and participated in infrequent exceptional acts of brutality. It has been assumed that Napoleon actually suffered from a bipolar disorder, but there isn't much evidence supporting this claim. This nevertheless is thought to have been his driving factor underlying his rule as he was violent and behaved very poorly. His intellect is also attributed his intense bipolar disorder. He has also been reported as suffering from depression as his army was badly reduced as he invaded Russia. He had too much optimism in his troops resulting in him being disappointed as they didn't deliver. With his impact on Europe, Napoleon is fondly remembered.

His techniques in military operations have been examined at most military schools around the globe. He was also famous for the Napoleonic Code, it laid the foundations for judicial rule and government in many Western European countries. One author wrote that the arrogance of Napoleon was a consequence of his inferiority complex, and that because of of his lack of height, he took up intense aggression in order to offset for his fragile self-image. Long after the death of Napoleon Bonaparte in British custody on St. Helena Island, discussion has raged widely over his true cause of death.

Nelson Mandela

(1918 - 2013) President of South Africa, anti-apartheid activist

Nelson Mandela's slow journey towards the role as the South African President from being an Apartheid inmate, created a state and encouraged the world. He managed to reach out to the very same individuals who imprisoned him and dehumanized black people, thus he reached his goal for "true reconciliation" within what has always been, an emotionally traumatized country.

South Africans voted for Mandela as the country's first black President four years after his release, just one year after he obtained the Nobel Peace Prize. His easy way and understanding of language and symbolism resulted in preventing a significant racial discrimination. Maybe one of Mandela's greatest moments as a symbolic figurehead was when drank tea with the widow of an apartheid leader. Mandela continued to be the overarching signifier in a nation still fraught with racial tension and profound inequality till the time of his death. Mandela established the first black legal firm in Johannesburg in 1952 as an activist since he was a student at Fort Hare University. In 1961 he became head commanding officer of Umkhonto we Sizwe "Spear of the Nation", a group within the African National Congress as an armed underground division. He was arrested and imprisoned in 1964 during the so called; Rivonia tribunal, where he gave a speech and became an known symbol of the anti-apartheid struggle. Mandela was imprisoned 27 years on Robben Island. Political pressure on South Africa increased through most of his imprisonment. Mandela's administration will not be known for significant political accomplishments like that of US President Abraham Lincoln and the reign of British Prime Minister Winston Churchill.

He continued to serve only a five-year term, and following his retiring in 1999, he invested a lot of his energy in resolving disputes, particularly in the war in Burundi, despite his growing physiological fragility. Having been forced to see his children grow up during his time in jail, Mandela spent much of his time trying to improve young people's lives by trying to generate money from companies for education in remote locations. Mandela died at home at the age of 95, in Johannesburg, following months of medical attention for a respiratory infection.

Nikola Tesla

(1856 - 1943) Inventor

Nikola Tesla was truly one of the world's most groundbreaking inventors. Until encouraging the name of a series of environmentally-friendly vehicles, Nikola Tesla was indeed a significant innovator who, initially and despite due to his competitor Thomas Edison being moved to the fringe, achieved in creating technological developments far beyond his era. Sadly, he would not come to see everything his ambitions realized into. The conceptual "Death Ray" system, identified as the "Teleforce" by Tesla, would concentrate an electrical charge of energy and flow across the atmosphere.

If used successfully, Tesla figured it might e able to remove a fleet of 10,000 enemy aircraft inside of 200 miles of a defending nation's borders and effectivley stop military forces dead in their tracks. The inventor, with his odd sleep patterns, chose only two hours of sleep a day, but that was not the weirdest thing he would do. It has been said that often he would curl his own toes 100 times on each foot before he would finally go to bed at night, because he felt that his brain cells as such were enhanced. He loved to have pigeons near him, but he disliked gemstones and obese women. Nikola Tesla is one of the true heroes of technology. But during his scientific journey, Tesla was not only obsessive. He was probably suffering from a compulsive disorder (OCD), which made him refuse to touch something even slightly dirty like hair, pearls, earrings or anything with a round shape. He was also fascinated with number 3, 6 and 9 and went around a house three times every time before he could enter. And he would use precisely 18 napkins at every meal to clean the cutlery until they really sparkled. He was a trailblazer in many areas and his perception included exploring solar energy and sea power. He also mentioned interplanetary and satellite connectivity. His work has brought advancement in communications, lighting, lasers, radar, x-rays and robotics.

Despite Tesla's genius, he often fought powerful businesses and government officials. He was not recognized and died in January 1943, as a poor man. When he died, the government stole his work, although they later issued it back to his family. To date, the US Government even now classifies some of his documents as secrets.

Oracle of Delphi

Prophetic advisor

Ancient Greece was a men's country. Men occupied top positions in government, men died fighting on the field of battle and men governed the most powerful civilizations. But all these people, from the lowest countryman to the monarch himself, attempted to get one person's council and guidance— and that individual was a female. Pythia, also referred to as the Delphi Oracle, was perhaps the most highly regarded and intellectually rigorous oracle of the Greeks. By the 7th century BCE, Delphi was the hub of the world and a mighty temple over many years. A single individual who was selected to act as the link between our and the other world act as a bridge.

Before a consultation with Delphi's oracle, no significant choices were made by the rules of the day. It was not only the Greeks, and also foreign officials, politicians and monarchs who went to Delphi to inquire of the oracle. Contact with a deity was not a simple case of small significance and not just everyone would be authorized or respected to fill this purpose. A perfect, virginal and truthful young girl was decided to be the vessel most suitable for this spiritual role. There was nevertheless one disadvantage: fine young virgins were likely to attract unwanted attention from the males who pursued their advice and oracles were abused and harmed. Older ladies of at least 50 years of age started filling the role and they'd dress in the old virgin clothes to recall what was once. Being an oracle had an essential and vital role to play–one which fully embraced the self as becoming a myth. To the Greek society, Pythia was so essential that a completely empty slate was needed, so that kids, spouses and all ties with past life must had to severed for divine service of Apollo. One hypothesis is that its oracular influence was derived from Kerna waters of the spring flowing beneath the temple. Another proposition is that Oleander, the toxic plant, was the natural consequence of their prophetic abilities. Among the most common arguments to justify the oracles is, of course, that they actually faked their prophetic visions.

Due to the power their predictions might carry, the clerics or the females themselves abused that authority, as they saw appropriate. Either way, through her recommendations and proposals she exerted significant influence over the wealthy and powerful throughout antiquity.

Pablo Picasso

Picasso was possibly one of the most influential figures of culture and artistic revolutions of the 20th century. By the age of 50, as a Spanish painter he would become the most successful artist in contemporary art, with a distinctive visual style. Until Picasso there were very few painters who really had an influence on the world of art, and therefore he had a great deal of followers and was praised as being unique. The capacity of Picasso to generate works in a variety of styles has rendered him well honored during his own life. His reputation as a painter and influence of other artists indeed has only increased since his death in 1973.

He was certainly bound indefinitely to be one of the biggest artists in the world and in the history of mankind. When his seven-year old sister died, of the disease diphtheria in 1895, Picasso and his loved ones were devastated. They moved to Barcelona and his dad started working at the Fine Arts School. He encouraged authorities to allow his son to take the entrance exam, despite the fact that Picasso was dyslexic. After the first two tries he finally passed the test and attended art school, Picasso was only accepted at the young age of 13. Picasso underwent a bout of depression in 1901 and persisted with such suffering during various periods throughout his life. The major depressive episode started after a friend's suicide. During that following year, his depression exacerbated. His work was significantly impacted by his mental condition; he used only shades of green and blue and paints dull subjects like sex workers and homeless people. Picasso's entire career exercise was immense, stretching from the early years of his adolescence unto his death, providing a much larger history of his advancement than any other painter. The free spirit of Picasso, his excellent attitude and his utter ignorance of what others felt of his creations and his innovative practice rendered him an inspiration for countless other artists. Pablo Picasso died of pulmonary oedema and severe heart failure in France, on 8 April 1973.

Also regarded as the true father of modern art, every significant artist or art movement that preceded him was influenced by Picasso's authenticity. His life and creations are still inviting numerous academic definitions and attracting multitudes of people all over the world.

Philip K. Dick

(1928-1982) Author

American US science fiction author whose books and short story collections frequently depict the mental struggles of protagonists caught in illusions. Dick's artistic range and prominence saw him in a 30-year period write over 40 books and 121 short story collections. Dick was an unwelcome boy growing up in Chicago in the 1930s. Some boys threw rocks at him while he was hiding under cars, growling as if he was a dog.

Working decades in cycles of several days of writing and sleep crashing, after energizing on stimulant splurges which obviously took a beating on his body. There are a few suggestions that Dick had hallucinations and mystical premonitions long before a well-known nervous breakdown during a period in the seventies. In a 1965 article he addressed his own schizophrenic symptoms. He assembled an 8,000-page collection of personal notes recording his imaginative encounters, not least the extent to which he pursued various state of minds as a prize-winning author, gnostic deity and time-continuous heretic. In mid-1970, Dick said he had discarded the stimulants as e saw them as unnecessary, but not before among other things, they allowed him to believe in inter-dimensional entities during a series of delusions. In his later works, Dick discussed this and his rehabilitation from drug use, such as within the paranoid work "A Scanner Darkly" dystopia. Dick's research also discussed psychological, spiritual, religious, political and social concerns with a special emphasis on altered consciousness experiences, substance usage, transcendence, mental illness and the true nature of our reality. Many of Dick's tales reflect on the nature of existence and the sense of individual identity which often transforms into delusional hallucinations.

Because the characters sometimes realize that the reality they think is a real, indeed is an illusion put together by external forces. The works of Philip K Dick have become several hit films, such as "Blade Runner." The movie Total Recall," the "Minority Report" and "The Adjustment Bureau"
all include creations and adaptations of Dick's work. Dick lived as a poor man with little intellectual prestige outside of the science fiction
community following years of heavy drug abuse and serious mental illness. Nevertheless, he was generally considered a master of inventive dystopian literature by the end of the 21st century. When it comes to saying "he was ahead of his time" indeed without doubt he has seen unlike anyone else before him, the ramifications of the modern world, the worldwide success of industrial might, the rise of today's multinational technocratic societies and the dissociation in digital media.

Plato

He has created major areas of philosophy such as epistemology, ethics metaphysics and aesthetics. Plato was an ancient Greek philosopher and mathematician. His work paved the way of research, Western philosophy and natural philosophy. Throughout his Socratic dialogues he was a very articulate author. He used his dialogs to teach rhetoric, philosophy and logic. Plato was also assumed to have been trained by the best people of the day in both music as well as gymnastics. Plato also travelled extensively in Cyprus, Egypt and Italy, and only moved to Athens when he was 40 years old. Plato founded the first well established formal academic institution on a large parcel of land.

Plato was always active in Syracuse political affairs. While Dionysus became emperor, he is said to have toured Syracuse. He was the quintessential moral philosopher whose theories had a profound influence on the political theory which developed during his lifetime and well beyond his death. Plato and Aristotle, each produced a work of political philosophy, Plato created the Republic while Aristotle created the concept of politics. The Republic is focused on the creation of an ideal state and the manner in which humans can create a perfect society. Plato envisioned humanity should remove the need for a family and dismantle the need of private property and the familiar conventions of owning anything even individual gender roles as personal ownership was by him perceived to be the cause of all problems in society at large firmly rooted in selfishness of the individual. An ideal state would flourish when egocentric arguments against social unity were dealt with and replaced with the ideal of mankind's nature. Plato did not consider democracy the best form of government. Firstly, although freedom is for Plato a true value, democracy involves the danger of excessive freedom, of doing as one likes, which leads to anarchy.

Secondly, equality, related to the belief that everyone has the right and equal capacity to rule, brings to politics all kinds of power-seeking individuals, motivated by personal gain rather than public good. Democracy is thus highly corruptible. It opens gates to demagogues, potential dictators, and can thus lead to tyranny. A few of Plato's students were ultimately turned into Greek city-states becoming rulers, counselors and political advisers. Aristotle was his most famous student. Plato is rumored to have suffered from bipolar disorder, which at that point may not have been understood. Plato was a shy person, very little outspoken. He became aggressive when he practiced wrestling. He was also supposedly upset after Dion of Syracuse subjected him to slavery and was incarcerated. He felt betrayed and indignant. He generated the forms that he said are the conceptual representations of the property types we see. Platonism comes after Plato as a term that applies to the rejection of the real world. Plato, though claiming that there is another universe beyond material things, understood the complexity of the material world. Those who reject the material world and common truth are said to be platonic. Plato was eventually murdered. In 347 B.C.E. Athens turned away from its political and territorial aspirations during his existence and became Greece's cultural hub.

Pythagoras

(570 - 495 BC) Philosopher and mystic

A Greek mathematician who is regarded among the most important authors to quantitative reasoning. His principle has been used not only in geometry and trigonometry, but also in efforts to decode creation and to construct a progenitor of physics. Pythagoras was also one of philosophy's most famous thinkers. It is claimed so because he was the first man who called himself a "philosopher." He was also the leader of Pythagoreanism, which was a religious and political organization. Like Socrates, Pythagoras has not left any document behind and that is the primary reason we do not know much about his experience.

Many ancient historical personalities, including Plato and Aristotle, told some details about the theory and philosophies of Pythagoras. He moved to Italy where he established a school whereby his students were told that numbers were the core of the whole world, and that these figures should also be venerated as such. He was one of the founders of vegetarianism, but he rejected eating beans through his commitment to this rigid lifestyle. Pythagoras had no affection of beans and vegetables, so far as any of his disciples were forbidden from consuming them or from handling them. It is uncertain whether or not this dislike for beans was due to health factors. He said that you never could consume fava beans since they bring you gas, and expulsive gas takes away the "breath of life." At the very same time, he believed that the souls of the deceased were held inside fava beans. He was extremely strict with regard to sex. Body fluids, it seems to Pythagoras, were components of the soul of a man. He claimed a man gives up some of his force when his fluids are removed from them. The disciples of Pythagoras were instructed to abstain however possible from sex. The disciples of Pythagoras literally thought he was a god's son. They also felt that it was because of his mathematical capacity.

Pythagoras once said he had incarnated many times, among other items, and he was the son of Hermes who gave him the power to recall to whom he was in all his past lives. No matter whether you think Pythagoras's beliefs were sacred numbers, gender ideals, or holy beans, his thoughts and mathematical concepts continue to be made compulsory around the globe. Pythagoras is believed to have died at the age of 75. A variety of ancient sources say that he lived to be 100 and that he died of hunger after he didn't eat for 40 days.

René Descartes

(1596 - 1650) Philosopher, mathematician, and scientist

Philosopher Rene Descartes of the 17th century shaped our thoughts in innumerable ways. The theory of dualism, the notion that the body and mind were entirely separate and distinct, was one of his greatest contributions to humanity. As shown by Descartes, the mind is completely abstract, and our human ability to think and to reason is also not linked to our physical existence. Cartesian doubt is a formal cycle of uncertainty, or doubt over the validity of one's convictions, which in philosophy became a standard method of thought. In addition, many have considered the Descartes technique to be the origin of the modern scientific method.

René Descartes popularized this form of questioning in Western philosophy, which attempted to doubt the validity of all his convictions, so as to assess that belief systems are valid. This is the reason for the argument of Descartes, "Cogito ergo sum," which mean; "I think, therefore I am." With both the task and process for putting all knowledge together for a number of years, within a modern global scientific "wisdom," Descartes viewed the vivid dreams he had on night of the St. Martin Vigil as a message from God himself. From that point on, Descartes thought he had a divine authority to create a systematic science of human knowledge. Most specifically, he presented a new concept of the natural world that tends to influence our thinking today: a system of matter with several fundamental properties and activity of interaction with our minds according to a set of universal laws. The physical world comprised an abstract consciousness directly linked with the brain of human beings; Descartes thus coined the contemporary version of the mind-body problem we struggle with today. The heated debate on dualism vs naturalism, most of his peers agreed with him on the matter. In hundreds of years to come dualism became widely accepted with a major impact on the view of religion, psychology, culture and morality that can still be witnessed today.

In some ways this dualism has influenced clinical practice in mental health services, and physical health services later on as doctors continue to distinguish between mind and body in treatment from either a holistic or deterministic approach. This dualism also creates boundary lines between mind and body. René Descartes died of pneumonia at the age of 53 in Stockholm on February 11, 1650. He was at the time in Stockholm to support the Queen of Sweden in the creation of a research academy.

Richard Wagner

(1813 - 1883) Conductor, Composer

Wagner was quite a German composer, director of theater and conductor He was mainly regarded for his music dramas and operas. Wagner was marked by diplomatic isolation, tumultuous romances, poverty and frequent escape from his lenders during his final years. Several of the disciplines throughout the 20th century can track the effects of his ideals and its presence stretches beyond composition to performance, politics, literature, fine arts and drama. Wagner displayed surprisingly no musical skills and passion as a kid, rendering him one of the few of his siblings not to obtain any piano lessons.

His creations were later perceived as a threat to artists and audience safety as well as any culture which tried to maintain order. His music was not only seen as a sign of the physical and sexual pathologies synonymous with an anxious modernity, ranging from mental distress and degeneration to fatigue and perversion, but also as the actual source of them. It was also a period when the healthcare industry claimed that illness was caused by an unrhythmical body, while the wellbeing was seen as rhythmic. In reality, Friedrich Nietzsche, one of Wagner's once most enthusiastic friend and associate, issued a devastating judgement on the health dangers posed by his German colleague: in his 1888 novel, "The Case of Wagner," he launched the tirade and asked: "Is Wagner actually a man? Is he not rather a disease?" Music and the Holocaust combine in that shadow: one of man's most wonderful things, and some of the worst things that humans have ever achieved. Adolf Hitler had been inspired by Wagner, as the mad genius, even if he was deceased when the 12-year old Hitler first experienced his music live. Hitler reportedly stated: "Whoever wants to understand National Socialist Germany must know Wagner." You hear Wagner and become intrigued, shocked, captured and thrilled.

The Nazi period lay like a dark glow over the history of a great Germany, a land of composers, writers and thinkers who, in the 18th and 19th centuries, brought the world so much grace and color. Wagner suffered greatly from angina and died of a heart attack as he toured Venice in February 1883.

Robert Schumann

(1810 – 1856) Composer

He was a strange, troublesome genius and has written many of the finest Romantic pieces of music, and some of the least popular. Throughout his depressive spells he became significantly affected by something that was most likely a bipolar disorder yet he displayed nearly incredible performance. Robert Schuman is among the most famous composers of the 19th century. Schumann introduced a revolution in the broader world of entertainment during his career, working to fight for the rights of young talented artists. While he made a significant and impressive contribution to classical music, Schumann was sadly, one of the most underappreciated classical composers.

Schumann struggled with depression and even as so results of his works were often marked by pure insanity. His music however was incredibly open one of the very few who attempted to include autobiographical elements, concise names and courses. Schumann's family and friends worked hard to create an impression of him that played down the importance of psychiatric illness throughout his life. The popular perception was the extreme opposite. This idolized yet damaging effect of his final years in asylum described his idiosyncrasies as evidence of his insanity. At the end of the day, Schumann's prestige was generally reduced, his compositions tainted with his wickedness. He had attempted suicide several times in the 1830s, and he endured regular episodes of severe depression and emotional fatigue. Schumann became disproportionately distraught and encountered his first instance of manic depressive disorder, which prompted him to attempt suicide in 1833 for the very first time. The winter of 1854 saw a spectacular expression of Schumann's insanity: he encountered "angelic" noises, which rapidly turned into a bestial tone of "tigers and hyenas." On a bridge over the Rhine on a morning of February, he threw himself in the water; fishermen saved him. Even though he had a history of depression at a period when mental disease was widely misunderstood his world was quite disturbed.

As more of a critic, in some assumptions he was exceptionally clever, completely out of touch while in others view he was generous in every case. He was never a brilliant pianist, a conductor's disappointment and at times he wasn't even a really successful writer. But his whole being would be music, imagination and dreams. Schumann had been in a mental asylum during the last two years of his life. Yet he dedicated himself willingly, and he healed to a large extent early on. He joined the sanatorium of Dr. Franz Richarz and lived there until the age of 46 before he died on 29 July 1856. He was always passionate, always searching for the dream, the archetypal love song. The blend of poetry and creativity typical of his songs, which never has again been achieved always draws artists and audiences, which can be seen in the many festivals and concerts that play his creations.

J. Robert Oppenheimer

(1904 - 1967) Theoretical physicist

As the key figure behind the atomic bomb development. Four explosives had been produced under Oppenheimer's guidance and two of them were used during the end of World War II. On 6 August 1945 the United States discharged a first atomic bomb at Hiroshima. It is believed that almost 150,000 people were killed in Hiroshima and almost 80,000 were killed in Nagasaki. The narrowing of a conflict which might have lasted longer, with millions of casualties on both sides, inevitably had a short-term effect.

Another effect was the primary question of who should manage the nuclear arms, how many and whether modern, more dangerous forms of nuclear weapons should be produced. Oppenheimer objected that the much deadlier hydrogen bomb was being produced. The dispute persisted for decades after the Second World War. Oppenheimer had been doing his work for the military effort, while his sacrifices to the world were destructive, it wasn't like he was just trying to kill others in cold blood. The development of a nuclear bomb wasn't just a physics problem. This would be a unique engineering challenge and one which has to advance while fundamental theoretical problems remained to be solved. He always bore traces of a disturbed, impulsive rich boy, whose unhappy conduct often transformed into a miserable one. Sometimes he even appeared crazy. Oppenheimer would have a issue with one of his teachers as an university student. In the expectation that the professor could take a chunk, he wanted to lace an apple with arsenic and place it on the professor's plate. Ultimately, his scheme had been uncovered and it almost disqualified him, but the power of his family was strong enough both to avoid a murder charge and to keep him at school, yet he was forced to undergo therapy sessions.

Robert Oppenheimer, was a scientist who was bilingual and involved himself in a wide range of skills, including linguistics and philosophy. Oppenheimer's anxiety about the population's lack of scientific understanding and the challenge of communicating the nature of scientific advances to even informed lay people, together with the excitement of his imaginative inventions, contributed to several influential scientific articles. On 18 February 1967, Oppenheimer died of cancer of the throat.

Roger Bacon

(1220-1292) Philosopher and theologian

Roger Bacon was an intellectual and Franciscan friar, a brilliant natural scientist who was one of the founders of the "scientific method" and is well regarded for his use of quantitative experimental procedure. Bacon was conceived into an affluent family, he was fascinated and enjoyed the benefits of an early education in geometry, astronomy, music and arithmetic. His greatest achievement was "Opus Major," which included alchemy, optics and astronomical experiments. He also worked on hypotheses about the location and measurements of celestial bodies.

While upholding the Christian faith, Bacon claimed that a more objective scientific interpretation of existence was of great importance and believed that his ideas were of great significance to the benefit of the church as well as the universities. He was the very first person to explain the manufacture of gunpowder in detail, and he discussed motorized or moving machinery and wagons. Opus majus was also an attempt to convince the Pope of the desperate need and the extensive effectiveness of the improvements he suggested. Yet Pope Clement's death in 1268 destroyed his hope of gaining the proper place in the college curriculum of science Bacon as he pointed out himself with pleasure, showed tremendous enthusiasm and energy for empirical science, after all his research had been discussed all around and quickly gained him a place as some kind of prolific man in contemporary literature. Bacon was also one of the great Middle Ages rationalists. Chastising everything including scholasticism, the Julian calendar, even to acknowledging Catholic doctrine and Church authority. A further major shift happened in Bacon's career in 1257. Bacon felt ignored by everyone except the dead, because of his ill health and his admission into the Order of the Friars Minor. He seems to have accomplished his career and writing profession.

His febrile effort, his excessive skepticism, his magical thinking, his overt disdain for all those who did not share his desires frustrated his superiors and put him under strict supervision. The wrath of the ecclesiastical government was ignited by Bacon. In 1279, as he was too creative as a philosopher, he lived the remainder of his life strongly shackled in a Franciscan cathedral. He eventually and sadly died there in captivity, a true martyr of free thought.

Salvador Dali

(1904 - 1989) Artist

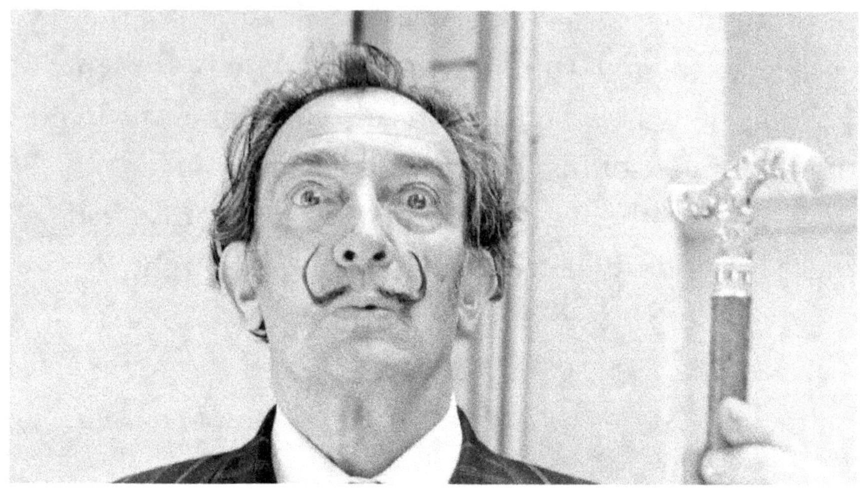

Dalí, an eccentric childhood figure, liked to push the limits of his personal and professional life. But he was also a self-promotion huckster and master. Though grotesque, Salvador Dali's originality arises unwittingly from his creation. Salvador Dali was born in Spain in 1904 and was named after his elder brother who died a short time before his birth. The memory of this late brother whose life Salvador felt was stolen would always come to affect his future. Salvador has been haunted since childhood by the strong yet clouded presence of a lot of social anxiety and phobias which would drive him into his dream world to show his talent for artwork.

At the age of seven, he created his first painting. Furthermore, Dali characterized himself as twisted and as a child dedicated himself to weird pleasures to be judged by most people. For instance, he used to revert to isolated activities, urinate his bed purposely and commit exhibitionism without shame to disturb his subordinates. Intrigued with Freud's philosophy, Dali preferred to merge his creativity with his passion for the dream world. He soon realized that his works were successful if he had his own uniqueness and painted arrogantly with his vivid, abstract creativity. Until creating his own style, Dali tried to enter many cultural experiments which makes it impossible to identify him as a popular artist. Material on his conduct and paintings comes from different outlets, including his autobiography; literary texts; informal interviews with acquaintances, families and the performer himself; letters; and family history information. Here quite a systematic assessment experiment was undertaken, in addition to a concise review of such results, to determine that Salvador Dali seems to have had a personality disorder and was found to fulfill the diagnostic criteria of psychotic illnesses. Salvador Dalí is among the best-known artists ever.

His ferociously creative yet extremely unusual artworks, sculptures and pioneering adventures in film and interactive art during his life have led to an imaginative newer generation of expression. Only Leonardo da Vinci can line up his claim as a man who regarded himself as a genius. Until he died in 1989, he built an impressive legacy not only of his most popular Surrealist paintings but also of carvings, motion picture, photography and much more.

Sigmund Freud

(1856 - 1939) Neurologist and founding father of psychoanalysis

Sigmund Freud was a neurologist from Germany, who is perhaps better known as the father of psychoanalysis. Freud also developed a wide range of psychological approaches based on talking therapy, including methods such as transference, free association and dream analysis. In early days of psychology, psychoanalysis became a prevalent school of thought and continues to remain very influential today. Freud's philosophies have pervaded modern culture and theories such as freudian slips, denial, unconsciousness, wish fulfillment and the ego, are used in everyday language, as well as in modern fields of psychology.

He concluded that not all psychological diseases are caused by genetics and proved that differences in culture have an effect on psychology and our actions. His studies have helped clarify
our personality, clinical psychology, development of human and pathological psychology. He had a profound impact on our shallow sexual understanding of the self. Yet his therapy sessions ignored ethical codes and sometimes distorted information to meet his objectives. Nevertheless, he brought into the public consciousness the idea of unconscious mind. The individual himself was an eccentric whose personality was as strange as his convictions. While Freud was a young medical student in Berlin, he studied the effects of cocaine on the mind and body and wrote a number of papers about its health benefits in his lifetime. However, he named himself his favorite test subject of cocaine. From a young age to 83 years of age, Freud was a tobacco man all the way through the development of cancer, and even remained a smoker despite of the cancer eating through his jaw. Although he was hospitalized and underwent surgery multiple times, Freud could not restrain himself from his love
of cigars. It is said that Freud consumed twenty cigars a day. He claimed addictions were only a normal sex patterns and kept his family and friends in the dark regarding his illness.

But he could not hide it anymore as he started wearing a prothesis brace that prevented his jaw from fracturing. The research and teachings of Sigmund Freud led to influencing our understanding about infancy, temperament, memory, orientation and counseling. Many great thinkers also added to Freud's research, while others have developed new concepts out of disagreement with his concepts. With the aid of Physicist Max Schur and his daughter Anna, Freud got three lethal doses of morphine into his body and on 21 September 1939 and collapsed into a fatal coma. Two days later, his heart stopped beating.

Srinivasa Ramanujan

(1887 - 1920) Mathematician

Srinivasa Ramanujan was a mathematician who worked in England during the British rule of India. Even though he had hardly any formal education in mathematics, he contributed significantly to mathematical analysis, number theory, infinite series and continued fractions. Originally Srinivasa Ramanujan conducted his own mathematical work in seclusion; he gradually became recognized among Indian mathematicians. Ramanujan gathered almost 3,900 results separately, mostly identities and equations.

His initial and somewhat unorthodox findings, such as the prime of Ramanujan, theta function of Ramanujan and partition formulas opened up entirely new fields of study and stimulated a great deal of science. He has become one of the youngest Royal Society fellows and only the second Indian and the first person to be elected as a Trinity College Fellow at Cambridge. The tuberculosis and vitamin deficiency of Srinivasa Ramanujan was diagnosed and he was confined to a sanatorium. The representation for abstract insight is iconic of Ramanujan. His story is a brilliant reminder of how mathematical vocabulary is written into the minds of everyone. Unlike Mozart, this young Indian had the ability to develop mathematical formulas by which he attempted to explain the universe. Obsessively observing his research: he would work 30 hours straight and sleep 20 hours consistently before working again. The approach of Ramanujan: imaginative and without structured presentations, contrasted with the form of scientific research that needed the replicability of results which is to suggest that another mathematician might adopt the methodology. The mathematician once said that Namagiri, his family's guardian deity, showed him in visions the equations of his calculations.

Contrary to expectations, his wellbeing in his homeland deteriorated steadily and only lived until 26 April 1920, when he died of a combination of illness and severe malnutrition. He published a variety of notes and papers with almost 4,000 results and conjectures before he died. Ramanujan was a blessing for science and mathematics. Many of the obscure calculations he documented in his dismal journals have influenced our present and future sciences. While in England, there is no official medical history to retrospectively identify Ramanujan's disease, several written reports raise questions about the accuracy of a simple case of tuberculosis as the cause of his death.

Stephen Hawking

At age 21 Stephen Hawking a theoretical physicist became diagnosed with ALS, a condition that causes muscle weakness and then paralysis. Two years to live were given to the young man whose talent was already evident. Hawking lived against all expectations for further than 50 years. Asking how his disease had developed so dramatically than in the majority of cases, Hawking told a medical journal that motor neuron dysfunction may have different causes as his condition might have been due to a lack of vitamins. He was the first person to establish a concept of cosmology described by a combination of general relativity and quantum mechanics.

As a theoretical physicist, researcher and cosmologist at the Center of Theoretical Cosmology he became admired for his work. Hawking, as a young man, researched general relativity and how black holes were created. His knowledge of geometrical methods enabled him to prove a number of extraordinary theorems about the conditions under which spinning clouds of matter collapse, forming gravitational singularities or black holes. The most prominent discoveries of Hawking are an equation providing the black hole entropy a measure of its intrinsic randomness and disorder. The observation that the entropy of a black hole relies on its area was a major scientific achievement by Hawking. This ensures that if something falls into a black hole, then it also expands its volume. This insight contributed to a paradigm shift: if a black hole can become entropic, it must also be able to emanate some of its volume back to the universe The idea of a gradually decreasing radiation in a black hole is termed "hawking radiation." Even after his language was impaired, he was always able to communicate by a voice amplifier, at first by using a portable device then finally with a single cheek muscle. He died at the age of 76 on 14 March 2018, after dealing with the illness for over 50 years. Stephen Hawking is a modern physics icon by all regards.

His efforts have improved our understanding of nature as well as encouraging thousands of scientists. Given the disease of Hawking, his work motivated generations of students to investigate gravity and quantum mechanical challenges.

Steve Jobs

(1955 - 2011) Entrepreneur and co-founder of Apple Inc

Looking into the man's history. After all, Steve Jobs reputation becomes even more remarkable as he is seen as one of the greatest famous people in technology history. Over the years, Jobs managed the advancement and huge success of the Apple services and products which gave solid financial gains for Apple. The company's revitalization is seen as one of the largest business recoveries in history. Steve Jobs was admired for a great deal: his technological ability, as a charismatic billionaire, a professional salesman, and for being and incredible jackass.

The universe of personal computers and cell phones has been revolutionized because of his work. As shown by his biography, while in the workplace he had a special way to alleviate his pressure. He would wash his feet in the toilets of the company. His diet had always been a strange thing. He was sometimes vegetarian and vegan, and for a while he was persuaded that his meat-free diet, of course free from contaminants, produced no body odor. He avoided simply showering or even using antiperspirant, not so much to the satisfaction of his colleagues Jobs despised the social construct, which is shoes. He often walked in bare feet around the office. Jobs had a mystical temper He became notorious for firing people for the least errors, both at Apple and in Pixar throughout his period. Jobs refused to recognize his daughter, Lisa, for many years. He also claimed that he was sterile and thus would not undergo a fatherhood examination. For Lisa and her mother, it was disgraceful as they struggled financially as the greatness of Apple began to grow. Jobs was treated in 2003 with pancreatic cancer. The great news was that it was a rare condition that was very useful and likely that he would rebound from it. But he strangely defied the diagnosis of the surgeon for much more than a year, trying to cure the cancer himself by taking healthy and natural drugs. He finally agreed to the procedure, but it was far too late.

Before he died in 2011, cancer would still cause a number of health problems for him. Steve Jobs might be dead, but he isn't overlooked. Still years after his death, the legend around the individual remains strong, he still occupies online debate, which is more prevalent than Tesla CEO, Elon Musk, Facebook CEO Mark Zuckerberg and Microsoft founder Bill Gates as according to Google Trends.

Vaslav Nijinsky

(1889 - 1950) Russian ballet dancer and choreographer

While barely known today, Nijinsky had been a household name in the early 1900s. Regarded to be the finest male dancer of his era, he was known for his intensive performances, huge leaps and the capacity to dance on his toes, something unusual for male professional dancers. As he choreographed ballets, his progressive approach to dance contributed to an uproar. Although Nijinsky was 26, his career was influenced by the effects of his illness.

He lived the remainder of his life into and out of mental institutions, sometimes going for weeks without saying a single word. He was obviously also an exceptional actor less realistic than classical Ballet had declined in Europe for over half a century and the traditional male choreography as an art was almost dead: in many other western ballet theatres, women often performed leading male roles. Nijinsky was also something completely unexpected, a blessing to his fans. His psychiatric biography in 1991 is hypothesized that through his mother the dancer might have been genetically predisposed to depression. After being widowed, she starved herself to death. He could also have had a possible brain damage from a crash which he suffered at the age of 12. In all situations, it is obvious that Nijinsky at least wasn't like most children in late teenage years. Even the biggest proponents to schizophrenia as a biological theory accept that constitutional insecurity must be coupled with some intense psychological stress to trigger the disorder whereas Nijinsky's later psychosis is likely genetically dependent. In the case of Nijinsky the biggest pressure is probably that he was unable to do what he regarded as his job, Nijinsky suffered his first nervous breakdown after he was fired from the Ballets Russes.

He could not sleep, he was afflicted with fears and he also became enraged, a condition likely aggravated by his increased responsibilities. Then he was sent to the Bellevue Sanatorium in Kreuzlingen, a lavish and compassionate institution operated by the father of existential therapy Ludwig Binswanger. In only three months Nijinsky was hallucinating, he pulled his hair out, his caretakers were attacked, and he declared that his extremities belonged to another person. Many of Nijinsky's works were simply an artist's creation. Health records of Nijinsky demonstrated some psychological progress until he died of kidney failure at age 60.

William Shakespeare

(1564 - 1616) Playwright and poet

Often named a national English poet, he was known by many as the finest dramatist ever. Some authors cross regional boundaries, but no living prestige of writers is comparable to that of Shakespeare, whose plays have been performed in almost every major language on every continent in since the late 16th and early 17th centuries. The works of William Shakespeare draw on Greek dramatic techniques.

Through his stories he exposes the viewer to a myriad of relatable characters, presenting diverse personalities, interwoven with moral dilemmas and abrupt story transitions. He mastered many different styles, comedy, history and tragedy often incorporating two or more topics into one piece. While William Shakespeare's plays are well known worldwide, the man's early life is still a mystery. Today we think of Shakespeare as a literary genius, a backbone of theater tradition, a talented writer and immortal lover of poems. Yet even Shakespeare's most famous modern devotees are doubtful to perceive him as a founder in modern medical science. Much less as a pioneer in forensic psychiatry. Difficult to believe, though, it was an odd time in US culture when William Shakespeare was seen exactly as such in law and in medicine. No earlier person was quoted as an expert on madness and mental function during the first century of Modern psychiatry more often than William Shakespeare. In large part during the 19th century, the influence of Shakespeare, his unparalleled influence, was interpreted as his ability to properly represent human nature in all its forms. He is known as a naturalist and scientific expert, as well as clinical officials at the time were attracted to him partially since he did not give otherworldly explanations as to why people would act as they did.

He gave some kind of humanistic, almost a scientific interpretation of human behavior which explains why people admired his work as being empirical. He is supposed to be someone who more comprehends why people do the things they do than anyone who has ever existed. As being one of the greatest thinkers of all ages, Shakespeare's plays inspired many aspects of modern culture, from theater and television to fiction, politics and even transforming the English language. William Shakespeare died on his 52nd birthday, 23 April 1616.

Vincent van Gogh

(1853–1890) Post-Impressionist painter

Today's physicians concur that Vincent van Gogh suffered from psychosis; a sentiment held by many medical professionals hundred years after his death. That is because there are a number of possible causes that seem to have driven Van Gogh to cut of his own ear in 1888 and injure himself with a self-inflicted gunshot in the chest with a pistol two years later. He was also diagnosed with a brain lesion that was compounded by a treatment used to enhance the visual appearance of certain bright colors, which culminated in epileptic seizures.

He also drank allot of alcohol which in turn aggravated his epilepsy, he drank in order to alleviate his depression and anxiety. He had also suffered from lead poisoning which resulted from his use of paint, which was why he also felt nauseous and anxious as he explained in a letter to his brother. Bipolar disorder, syphilis, borderline personality disorder, psychosis and schizophrenia are among the explanations discussed regarding his condition over the years. Eventually, doctors couldn't definitely identify the underlying cause of Van Gogh's condition, which in his last years contributed to several extended stays in mental hospitals, where he was often also deemed as hostile and very aggressive. Vincent was a well-known Dutch artist. While his works of art were not recognized in his life, he still managed to influence the world 20th century art. His career was distinguished by a number of physical and mental ailments. Van Gogh created more than 2,000 works of art, comprising of over 900 paintings and more than 1000 sketches and drawings. His works are one of today's most expensive works of art that are sold and collected. He would sit down and write for many hours, as seen in his correspondence with his brother though some 800 letters.

Historians of art that have examined his private letters have noticed that he endured very depressive episodes, followed by mania in which he showed great strength and determination for his work. The remarkable faith and profound humanitarianism recorded in his hundreds of insightful, knowledgeable and compassionate letters to his brother, should not be eclipsed by his famous and substantial mental health problems. That in his professional career Van Gogh appeared capable of completing so many masterpieces to become a leading artist of his day, it is a testament to his exceptional ability, focus and faculty of mind.

Virginia Woolf

Virginia Woolf had a number of emotional disruptions when she was a young girl. Until she was 3 years old, she did not learn to talk in complete sentences. Virginia Woolf recorded her memoirs, wrote articles, kept her notes and sketches of her novels and published works detailing her childhood trauma. One of Woolf's most substantial issue was that she was sexually abused as a youth, a fact her biographers barely mention. Her first traumatic moment happened when her mother unexpectedly died when she was just 13. Her dilemma was exacerbated by her beloved sister's death two years later.

Virginia had been heartbroken and experienced a number of nervous breakdowns. After her father died, she had another episode of depression. She resolved her tremendous emotional damage however and became a prominent British novelist. Her works are deemed as groundbreaking because they dig profoundly into a character's psyche to demonstrate what they feel and think. As a professional intellect, she wrote her novels and essays and had gained both critical and mainstream popularity. Woolf was a pioneer in her work of integrating feminism. Journalistic and didactic works of Virginia Woolf indicate that she made an important contribution to the growth of feminist thinking. She is among the most popular and influential women writers in literature. The eccentric nature of Virginia Woolf is what separates her works from other writers of her day. The unique features of her works, such as structure, characteristics and subjects, are challenging to imitate and strongly impress readers of her literary works. It is well known that many who followed her existence believe she had suffered from a bipolar disorder. Her writing was a genuine showcase of her need for an inner vent due to her chaotic life. Woolf's husband characterized her as fairly stable as she began to work on new projects. She then often moved through her writing to sojourns of excitable hypomania and paranoid delusions.

Depression, usually reached her at the point of revision. In her entire lifetime, although she suffered to cope with severe mental problems, she eventually took her own life in 1941 at the age of 59 when she drowned herself in a river near her home. Her works were very popular and won the hearts of her readers. She is indeed seen as being one of the greatest personalities at have brought innovation to the English language. She tends to be recognized as the best novelist writer in English.

Vlad the Impaler

(1428 - 1476) Prince of Wallachia

Vlad the Impaler, the Prince of Wallachia, was a gentle tyrant who controlled the Transylvanian Romanian region, terrorizing the hearts of all who tried to defy him. Vlad the Impaler however did not start by impaling men. Yes, as a child he was just Vlad III, the son of the Transylvanian ruler Vlad II Dracul. During a period of particular unrest Vlad was born in 1431. Since his father was called Dracul, which means "the dragon" he also got the name when he joined a Christian military order, sponsored by the Holy Roman Emperor.

Hence, he was initiated into the Order of the Dragon. Transylvania was often the center of unrest due to its proximity to Christian-ruled Europe and the other large Muslim-ruled Ottoman Empire. Vlad held a banquet welcoming all who wished to challenge him in order to assert superiority and consolidate himself as a feared leader. As they appeared, he stabbed them and impaled their bodies on tall wood spikes. The strategy seemed to work very well, so much that Vlad decided to enforce it on all that went against him. It was known at the time that 80,000 were executed and 20,000 more were impaled during his rule, including Saxon traders, Ottoman mutineers, and elusive prisoners of war. The Ottomans slowly gained traction and military gains and tried to take the crown from Vlad as they marched into the region to conquer it. Vlad the Impaler was captured, decapitated and as tradition states, flaunted straight to Constantinople to be shown over the city gates. Vlad Dracula is still regarded as a Romanian national hero, despite his terrible violence. He was also the last major leader of an autonomous Wallachia, and shortly after his demise the Ottomans brought people under their rule by passing legislation that would prohibit the construction of fortresses. Nevertheless, the castle of Dracula remains today as a symbol of an independent past and as a symbol of the incredible mark left by Vlad Dracula to his nation.

The book "Dracula" was written in 1897 by Bram Stoker. The idea of a person who would eat and consume human blood in the dead of night was so frightening that reviewers attributed to it "the most bloodthirsty book of the paralyzed century." Legend of Dracula in some places of East Europe, is depiction of a hero who battled against Muslims effectively. Yet in most countries he is only know as a bloodthirsty ruler of the past.

Vladimir Lenin

(1870 - 1924) Communist theorist, founder of the Soviet Union

Vladimir Lenin has changed the world's history and has affected billions of lives. He formulated, nourished and guided the revolution and orchestrated the seizure of control over the largest country in the world in 1917. He introduced a new social and economic order on a never before tried level. The U.S.S.R. was governed by the communist party, but its government did not claim that the Union of Soviet Socialist Republic was Communist, they said the U.S.S.R. was Socialist.

The Constitution and its laws were appropriate for democratic elections in all the regions, districts and cities of the Soviet Union republics and in the autonomous republics. Voting through universal suffrage was legally protected and anonymous. His Socialist system would eventually dominate almost half of the world, which included regimes in China, Cuba and Vietnam that still survive unto today. He would not live to see all of it. Throughout World War II, Nazi Germany would be defeated, U.S.S.R would gain nuclear weapons, and the Cold War was fought over the West for 40 years. His nation was also the first to send a person out into space. Early life of Lenin proves he was a man focused on improving society. Vladimir invested time as a young adult as a solicitor to be better able to serve the working class. The historical fact sheet of Karl Marx and Friedrich Engels encouraged him to dedicate his life to battling socio-economic inequality, as well as being motivated by the revolutionary ideas contained in the "Communist Manifesto." Both these things show that Lenin was a considerate person with a commitment to transforming the world's mentality. Under the power of his government he embraced wrath and rage. He had endured daily stress for 17 hours through a micromanaged staff and disagreement over trivialities.

He accused inefficient employees with being "saboteurs and loafers." Lenin, as a child, had common diseases at the period: typhoid, toothaches, pneumonia and a debilitating skin infection. Apparently, he was under immense stress, contributing to his depression, migraines and bad abdominal pain. At the age of 48, he was shot multiple times during an attempted murder. There was a hole through his collarbone after his heart was punctured. Another one was stuck in his neck. For the rest of his life, both bullets remained intact. Lenin made a strong imprint on the Russian nation through his rise to prominence and his reign as its leader He is regarded as the father of a revolutionary Soviet Union, as he was a ruthless deceptive leader who used socialism for repressing his citizens; he remains extremely controversial for his behavior as leader of the Bolshevik Party, and the gains or disadvantages they had to the Russian people are still being discussed today.

Winston Churchill

Winston Churchill, without a doubt, was one of Britain's most famous figures. Churchill was a strong leader, not only dealing with foreign challenges but also with his own mental health struggles. He lamented of his "black dog of depression" in his 30s to some of his friends. Winston Churchill was assumed to have suffered from a bipolar disorder due to a lack of familial loving touch. Later in life he stood and considered suicide in the House of Parliament. The black dog would follow him throughout his life. He was intimate during his occasional manic phases, but his emotions could change rapidly. He earned a lot during his life by writing books. His works have always been popular.

He kept writing even when he was Prime Minister and also began writing newspaper articles. During phases of great mania he continued to write all night, producing 43 books in addition to following through with his political tasks. Churchill has established himself well in the context of history and biography authorship, for which he won the Nobel Prize in literature. Winston Churchill was a successful British Prime Minister, as was found out throughout the Second World War in his command of the British Army. He managed to form a coalition government, and during the war together with the Soviet Union and the USA he creates a military force of Allied Powers, as he refused to surrender to Nazi Germany. Born on 30 November 1874, Churchill shares his birthdate with the author of the book which you are currently reading. At first, s a child Churchill had a much distress that didn't allow him to speak well, but he worked so hard to overcome it. Churchill was by nature defiant and self-reliant. It explained his poor school results, which he was disciplined for. He started his military career when he joined the corps at the age of 17. Over almost fifty years, he also occupied other political positions. His words influenced many people in his country and the nation was highly revered by Churchill. He was also a great political analyst, cautioning of Hitler's rapid increase of power.

Winston Churchill indeed by all regards is one of the twentieth century's most prominent leaders. His influence is pervasive in Britain's national psyche and raises respect from everywhere around the globe. Sir Winston Churchill died of a major stroke on 24 January 1965 at the age of 90. He got the first state funeral despite not being a member of the royal family.

Wolfgang Amadeus Mozart

(1756 - 1791) Composer of the Classical period

Mozart was an imaginative, intelligent, highly motivated and most notably very successful musician before he was ever recognized as a genius. Wolfgang Amadeus Mozart is regarded as one of Classical Era's most talented composers. More than 600 plays have been dedicated to him which have become some of the worlds, most famous piano, opera, chamber and symphonic orchestrations. From the very start Mozart had a natural passion for music. As he was five years old, he first wrote and also appeared playing before European royalty. He was assigned as court musician in Salzburg at the age of 17.

Mozart had been a true visionary. Beethoven was indeed also inspired by his music, and some of his early works mirrored the style of Mozart. Most writers mention Mozart's bipolar disorder and anxiety in their writings. He himself stated in some letters, that he was unhappy, tearful and distressed with mood swings. In several instances, he also mentioned that his involvement with composition decreased with older age. Mozart even claimed that he couldn't focus and lost energy and had extensive feelings of remorse. When we equate all of these signs, Mozart probably can be seen as having suffered from a severe depression according to the medical standards of today. There is evidence that even at times Mozart used to awake at 6 in the morning and kept working until 2 the following morning. He also penned inconsistent messages and used offensive language. Mozart also asked his wife, his friends, and his father for quite a lot of attention and as he couldn't withstand being alone. He had an explosion of anger several times, so he drank a lot as well. Mozart died when he was 35 years old on 5 December 1791. He actually became the most famous musician in the world while still alive, and all his artistic works have been hailed as masterworks. Mozart traveled around the world, wrote in abundant supply, remained an insatiable music student, studied and played with virtually all types of music.

In all genres of music, from symphonies, string quartets, ballets, concertos, and piano pieces, Mozart exerts the ultimate impact. He is definitely one of the world's best, if not the finest, artists ever was a creative, talented, inspired and, above all, very productive composer before he was recognized as a genius. Wolfgang Amadeus Mozart is one of the brilliant classical age composers. He has more than 600 compositions to his name that have become some of the most popular piano, choral, organ, opera and symphony compositions. Mozart had a passion for music from the very beginning. At the age of 5, he first composed and performed before the European royalty. He was able to play the violin and the piano. Mozart was appointed court musician in Salzburg when he was 17 years old. Mozart had been a genuine genius. Beethoven was also inspired by his work, it was said, and some early compositions of Beethoven reflected the style of Mozart. Many authors mention Mozart's bipolar disorder or depression in their papers. He said that he experienced sadness, tearfulness and a deprived mood in some of Mozart's letters. He also mentioned that his interest in composing had decreased in several places. Mozart also complained that he could not concentrate, lost energy and had guilt. If all these effects are combined with contemporary medical criteria, Mozart can be inferred from severe depression.

There is evidence that Mozart used to rise at 6 a.m. He kept working until 2 a.m. in the morning. He also wrote inconsistent letters and he also used inappropriate humor. Mozart always asked his girlfriend, his family, his dad for much attention and could not stand alone. He has demonstrated a temperate rage several times, and he too has a lot of alcohol. Mozart died when he was only 35 years old, on December 5, 1791. He became the most renowned musician within a short period of 35 years, with all his artistic works as masterpieces. Mozart has traveled throughout his life, abundantly composed, remained a voracious musical student, exploring and experimenting with virtually all kinds of music. Mozart's influence is supreme in all musical genres, from symphonies, concertos, operas, chamber music and solo piano. Without any doubt, he is one of the greatest or the strongest musicians ever.

The End

We must hold the memories of the culturally celebrated dead in reverence for their philosophy "love of wisdom", all that knowledge which resided within so many of the great minds that came before us. Their wisdom must weigh heavily on our own effortless suffering and progression through life. Likewise should humanity rejoice, in our collective strength of methodical considerations and struggle for solidarity, within both rational and irrational dimensions of human existence. Because it is thus that our common epistemological reflection of truth, also was carried with burden by so many iconic characters of our past. Without them the hallmarks of a truthful reality as we know it, would not have ushered in such a magnificent variety of emotional challenges and staggering accounts of personal self discovery. People around the world, should with respectful regard of these former tragedies, oppose the false legitimacy of institutions and actors which through the ages have solidified and entrenched their moral superiority in our minds.

We need to allow our understanding of our own psychological aberrations, as being predominantly implicated by the foundations of the structures of society and not merely as sourced through genetic inheritance, environmentally exposure or faulty brain chemistry. These malevolent forces of attitudes, have acquired their powers over the freedoms of all members of societies by way of systematic capitalization of our faculties of the mind and production of knowledge. Resisting and questioning the authority of these whom define our choices in our absence is paramount, they are the constitutive powers that work for the upholding of our ambivalence towards the false necessity of imposing the structures of economic and cultural capital on every human. They suppress the freedoms of creativity, productivity and neutrality in all fields of knowledge and ownership of free thought and self realization. These are the oppressors of factual information, unhindered by an illegitimate civic law and externalized ritual of persecution. The suffering voices of the majority of free minds, the low-income labour classes, remain until this day the most incarcerated target groups of any members of societies. In prisons worldwide, there are more than ten million people, many of whom live in dehumanizing detentions without trial.

Hundred of thousands of people, including leaders of unions, defenders and activists for human rights and investigative journalists thus remain missing. Hence throughout the ages, governments turned away from public punishment of the body and executions, they favoured erecting legislative structures that imprison the imaginative mind and disciplines the unresourceful body through class struggle. This is the neverending institutionalisation of fear against disobedient behaviours and its repercussions. As such, any state or government that manifests itself as being rightfully entitled of state ownership of self identity of its citizens, is misleading the marginalised masses within the framework of nationalised cognitive dissonance. Hence political exclamation of free choice and worthiness of resource distribution is nothing less of totalitarian inhumane mind control. The abstract cardinal stipulation of state fundamentality, is that the slavery of the personal mind is just and must remain a phenomenon hidden from the perception of its population. These false principles of social construction, concurrent with universal international agreements of human rights, should not be granted the supremacy of lawfulness as they seek only to supersede and undermine the adherence to free will of choice and dignity with the alternate state of mind.

Yet governments see it fitting, during times of both peace or war, to demolish the agency of freedom of particular thoughts and acts. We as populations are weakened by the inadequacy of motivation inherited in these laws, they waive our individual rights to self govern by proclamation of the protection of the suffering and unstable minds among us. The lie is being portrayed as the climax of universal moral values of majorities, with justifiable motives of cultural hegemony within governing authenticity. These prevailing norms of forced mental conditioning and indoctrination occurs utterly and foremost starting from birth in our involuntary dilemmas of structural arrangements, proceeding with family structures, marriages, glorified educational systems and fullness of the global free market competition. Our freedom has been conditioned to confine itself to the inferiority of expression within the enclosed vicinity of art, music and literature ever since humanity's dawn of historical enlightenment. These powers, aim at securing even deceitful democratic principles their dependence on our physical bodies, obliged into the labour forces we become less worth that the fossil fuel which powers their machinery of might and oppression. Our loyalty to their iron grip of power, through our consumer mentality in the distorted marketplace has turned us into economic zombies of usefulness.

Thus they continually restrain the collapse of their own progressive structural control and exercise of powers. They utter peace and solidarity, populism and nationalism, justaxposing these phony ideals to their delusive national borders and sharing of wealth and resources. They promise safety and empty moral codes together with baseless cultural values, as such they seek to derail our train of thought to make us concede to collective self-doubts and depression. Again and again they break their track record of intended stability and prosperity with shameful disregard for any compassion for our suffering. It should come as no surprise, that even those seemingly great nations managing the operating of somewhat healthy welfare systems, are quick to punish the poor and psychologically different people among us. Hence in the view of administrative powers, the value of the unresourceful citizens yields no return on investment, they have become no more than a retroactive burden on the system. Their freedom of mind deserves no time and space in the society they were born into, thus they are locked up under the pretence of safety and security for all or stigmatized unto the outskirts of city ghettos. These people represent the emergent fear of cognitive transcendence over certainty and pose a certain dismantlement of systematic governance.

They meet the true universality of truth of set criteria, as being the means to an end, whereby the fictional structures of law and order are seemingly perceived as necessary and vital for maintaining state-wide chronic disorientation of our minds through utilitarian ideals. The cost paid to fund society, is through the loss of personal freedoms of mindful experience of reality, this tension is fictitiously produced against the ideal of an ultimate collective quest for the meaning of life, one that nature intended us to follow. This is the ramification of artificial culture which unfolds within all of us, this is the subconscious conflict that arises through planning against the common good of our race, as so it shows its ugly face within all communities of fellow men and women which remain blinded to our tremendous development of cultural inequalities. The false narrative grows under the guise of intellectualism which does not want to assist us so we can thrive and not only survive, only within this regard have they managed to convince us that the cost of modernity outweigh the benefits of a free mind. These facts of life, allow for us to unconsciously refrain from an evolutionary altruistic mind-set of the many, while forcing us rather into devotion and admiration of the selfish agenda of the laws carved in digital stone by the few.

Those without compassion, which historically seized power and materialized these ideals as an intrinsic systems of state sovereignty, would be the one willing to wipe their bottom with the papers of constitutions in a state of emergency. Their false immutable benefits of emergent laws, underscores the entrapment of the self identity within the system ruled as lawful only for the greater good. Individualism has increasingly in the modern day and age destroyed the minds of the young, they chase affirmation and self worth based on the very foundations that others dictate as dictators of the necessary economic growth. Our minds have outgrown the inherent worth of our physical labor or that of any commodity within their marketplace. These puppets of boys and girls become delusional by the very system that they continually aid in upholding, for its unchallenged merit in claim of identification with our evolutionary needs is allreaching. It has evolved into a failure of our private lives, where only the strong minded survive as weak mindless participants. It is the neverending contradiction of the supply and demand of superficial knowledge and wisdom, it fuels the growth of a society wherein they play the game of life which strives only to addict their natural reward system.

Within these fanatic ramifications, the current prevailing reassurances of success of the innovative attention based economy, has utterly shown its true face of exploitation of our natural urges for social networks. These communities, have superseded all common sense of urgency for a self fulfilling authentic life. As young we become fostered with ever increasing levels of anxiety and mental disorders ramping out of control, their monopoly on free thought and expression, further confirms the need for our seductive labels of uniqueness and competitive influence among peers. These are the borderless confides of detrimental effects to our mental health decline which occurs in the vast population at large. It is thus paramount, that we as humans do not discredit the value of free conversation across all levels of society. The modern world of today is overwhelmed by its fear towards the multitude of public safety threats that seemingly appear abruptly, with instances of at times merely ambiguous indications of intent of violence carried out by perpetrators of mass shootings, terrorist actions and civil unrest. Sadly our advanced intelligence gathering has led to administrative technologies which offer the power elite an ever increasing level of sensitivity and specificity, this data is upholding their improper laws through early diagnosis of the labels of neuropsychiatric causes of violence.

What mankind fears, he blames on the unknown. We are collectively forced to allow the statutory systems the right of determination of our intent and purpose of actions with no basis in casualty. The controversial aims of enormous big data gathering and algorithmical artificial intelligence analysis of our patterns of our behaviour, grants the administrative powers extensive oversight and control of all aspects of our lives through extra-judicial Orwellian mass surveillance. The economic might of private ownership of these technological high castles are poorly differentiated between the public governance of good, versus the bad intentions of allowing them insight into our resources and access of mass extraction of our private consumer data with the aim of cooperating with preemptive crime prevention measures. There cannot be any understatement, regarding the threat such governance programs pose to civil liberties, with its ignorant argument of adhering to smart city planning and administration of collective resources. The unbelievable overreach of official institutions are at tremendous risk of imposing definitions of "mental illness" and "terror threat" by flagging of any individual for expressing their political beliefs or legitimate opposition towards official government narratives.

Such preemptive declarations, against any potentially violent citizens based on vague criteria stands to destroy the very fabric of civil society, the cornerstone upon which so many great thinkers built their ideals with their suffering agony and mental hardship. Despite the legacy of plentitude of these brilliant people, the world remains a staggering melting pot of human degenerative traits that daily reminds us, about the violent nature we are prone to in our treatment of each other. Concurrently, our animalistic tendencies continue to give rise to one of humanity's most serious historic challenges. Our evil and cruel behavior as natural born killers, manifests ongoing armed conflicts, crime, extremism, extrajudicial, sexual and gender-based violence which daily affects millions of people worldwide. We ought therefore to declare, that mankind's actions are never enfolded in a vacuum, but unfolds at all times within the ramification of the structures we have erected to govern us. The massive economic and social inequality which undermines fundamental human rights, are being celebrated by the powerful elites with self-interest of maximizing profits and abundance for the few as they fight us for control. The corrosion of democratic principles is staggeringly hidden from our perceptions through false legitime governance.

As such they sound the dishonest trumpets of global risks posed by technological advance and escalating climate threats while they act as the end is not in sight. Their agenda of recurring violence against our free minds is as such a masquerading showcase of good intentions aimed at safeguarding continued social disorganization, they are thus successful in enabling concentrated disadvantages by means of increased poverty, unregulated urbanization, rapidly growing unemployment and dismantling of social cohesion with the sole aim of safekeeping only their own beneficial Machiavellian security and justice institutions with self-serving impunity. Their impeccable argument for further expansion of these relative moral ideological structures, is a way paved with erroneous good intentions of ignorance, hence their growing capacity to analyze and interpret human behaviors under routine surveillance yields them the power of continued governing through professionalism of political standards. It is only by the lack of our critical supervision of their methods, that allows them to pass their agendas through electoral cycles. Thus as time progresses they manage to keep their stronghold on business as usual activities, boldly adhering to an intertwined reality of just necessity for judicial strength through economic growth and stability.

Regardless of diminishing and devastating effect that their resource mongering has on the global civil society at large. These selfish humans are foundational to the fabric of a web of lies and evil incarnations of moral ambiguities, they speak of improvement of communities of the future, yet they know their grip on power is confined to the mortal limit of their own deaths. They possess no whatsoever inherit ability to predict the needs of the many across the vast arrow of time. Hence, they rely on comprehensive development of governmental approach which are deemed as necessary, for preventing and reducing the effect of violence in their nations and abroad at any cost. They claim to fight for non-violent ideals, while alongside they continue building the architecture for ideological division and export of ethnic and religious conflict. They successfully practice their agenda and subjectively confound our minds with policing of inter-relational grievances, placing the blame on individuals and their lack of non-conformity. Our collective disbelief of the current situation, bears all the signs of oppression of our minds through institutional rights of ownership of truth. Central to the ascension of their power, remains the creation and cooperation between state and city authorities, the bureaucratic tunneling of powers across democratic enslavement of our identity.

It entails the rule of law and oppression of knowledge and intuition justified only as the necessity of capital allocation and structural integrity. The illusion of evidence-based authority, has managed to oppose personal freedoms and fully replaced our ownership of free thought with their partnerships of education and research institutes. Hence only they are forming the basis for an imposed factual need of improvement of mankind's inherit abilities for self-sovereignty, a destiny they claim is unachievable without their help. The devastating effect of these thought constructs, throws millions of people through criminal physical punishment and psychological suffering even in peaceful countries, the oppressors continue to justify this harm inflicted upon millions more which have their minds injured in occurrences of refugee displacement and forced migrations enabled solely through enacted willful warfare and regulated inter-national warfare. The violence inflicted on our mind is a fact of life determined by the choice of a few elected, they cause it to be and terminate its effect only when they see fit. As free minds we are forced to acknowledge that our will of action has vanished, even as quickly as we are allowed to vote and our own right of intervention is forever displaced through representatives.

Mind you, as the reader of this book, that without the eccentric and genuine transformations through mental struggles of our past heroes and benefactors of wisdom, even our modest achievements as a species would have been diminished and utterly shattered. As such the current societal stronghold of an all-consuming power over the masses, continues its grand theatrical act by manner of deception, undermining the very notion of creativity and productivity which they claim is a hallmark of only the successful few and healthy among us. The order of the day for elites, is to justify their continued claim of sovereign ownership of all knowledge, a restraint above the rest of us deemed as insufficiently normal or mature psyches. Regardless of the greater capacity of some of us, to dictate and reveal the yearnings for understanding and illumination of truth, through original knowledge and transcendent perception, we are nevertheless all forced to render ourselves to compete posed against each other, even until the day when we have made ourselves seemingly worthy of our pension and social mobility. There should be no doubt in the mind of the volatile consciousness of the weak and afflicted, that no human, organization or institution, of any prior adhered to foundational set of theories, have any universal right, either by law or by moral justification, to impose or restructure any physical or psychological borders on your mind.

As this is the neutral commitment of natural right to think, act and affirm your identity and individual freedoms, these indeed are wholly sacred, undivided and a legitimate autonoms force of nature, they are undoubtedly capable of questioning your rights. As a free agency of morality, a natural vessel of universal matter of fact, the dignity of every human being, has the claim to act as a sovereign state of mind, a composition of objective neutrality which is unbound by any other objects of stated false subjectivity. As such, the powers that be, have no right to oppose any of you own conflicting behaviors against you. Those whom are claiming superiority and obligation of duty of you, to conform and to forcibly choose, either between any good or bad ideals, or to make you feel that any of your choices are either right or wrong, they alone are in moral error. If society as a whole will not concede its powers, towards a fully direct democratic foundation, and a universal possession of political power and ownership of all intellectual property, whereby it is entitled to every habitant on this earth, with all the self representation of heroism within governance that must be bestowed unto them, then the right is your to revolt against their systematic rule.

Then this is your only duty, that as being of a higher order of fulfillment and enlightenment of a common universal ownership of equally and neutral aspiration for a shared authority, you must stand your ground as a witness, whereby observing the false governance of all international resources and knowledge are de facto precluding its own rights as the caretakers of citizenship. With the rise of clinical psychology in the twentieth century, the societal structures were granted legitimacy over our psyches, above and beyond our biological needs and necessities for innate capacity of freedom with the right of speech and act through self governance. Our misery and suffering continue to be blamed on our failing psychological narratives, yet the historic rebellion against the self is only enabled through pathological mental programs of nationalism and cultural identities. The power of our disenfranchised mind, is implicit from cradle to grave, the delusion is all encompassing and succumbs to a warped reality of our social contracts. Therein our sense of self has been removed from its true value, that as free humans we are the center of gravity among illusory material objects.

This unrealistic habitual reaction to reality, is continually imposed on our dysfunctional childhoods within the inherited framework of a systematic statehood, the false sense of mercy towards our parents, a phenomenon that is utterly impossible to reconcile or to be perceived through the veil of love of our offspring. Thus we are led to believe, that there is no way to become deconditioned and disassociate our minds from its grip of power over the nurture prohibiting our true nature. I the author, encourage you to embrace your unhappy discomfort of your freedom of mind. Hence you now stand at the ledge of the spiritual abyss of your own consciousness, it is your right and duty to tear down the dishonest and unreal abstract enclosure that society has erected in your thoughts through your distorted emotions. It is not by education or merit of work that humanity has advanced, it is through the legacy of those erratic, delirious and the crazy mad lunatics of yesterday by which the sun arises and something new envelopes our shared experience of today and tomorrow. They are the ones who walked through the unbalanced fires of dogma and repression, with an insane awe of personal misfortunes and maniacal servitude of a truth deemed worthy for us all. It is only they who guided the struggles of evolution for our physical equality and freedom of the mind.

They have prepaid the cost of our ascension of ignorance and deranged cognitive transgressions against the self. Let therefore no authority claim that they own your authentic freedom of action and thought, for it is the foundation upon which reality has been built, it is the home within each and one of us can feel safe and secure, this is not a peripheral imaginary place to the cannon of truth about reality, for its is the central tenet upon which the universe revolves only as emergent in your awareness and its own perceptions of itself. May you not lose the recognition of your brave ways, so you may not become blind towards your own relevance for our common good, for it is through the very act of detaching yourself from the attention of others with courage, that the needs of one or few, will embolden you also to be triumphant and find you solace and comfort of a neutral unity of mankind. Embark on this path of concealed discovery of truth, grasp your inner brainchild in your study of the self and you will manage to exercise the sensations of the very meaning of life in the quest for truth. The veil of conceit through opinion and impression, has kept hidden the intrinsic visualization of self realization from your knowledge in your convenient despair of mental blocks.

At last indeed you may feel that you also have the mandate and legitimacy to be cognizant over all of creation and existence of self, to acknowledge and discern your relative authentic place in space and time. Hence from this day, no man will have the force to judge you with their lives and laws, your freedom is the power set free to divide and sever the chains of their moral bondage, so even you alone and helpless may change naturally with the future of history. It is indeed your neverending time, to perpetuate and mind yourself, away and beyond the limits that have crushed your neutral roots of legitimate growth. Hence your name shall inevitability hereafter by divine moral universal decree, be worthy of a chapter, not merely doomed as a footnote in the book of life.

<When nobody owns anything everybody owns everything>

"No great genius has ever existed without some touch of madness." — Aristotle

www.ingramcontent.com/pod-product-compliance
Lightning Source LLC
Chambersburg PA
CBHW061332250726
48657CB00004B/1133